NOT FOR AMBITION OR BREAD

NOT FOR AMBITION OR BREAD

THEODORE DALRYMPLE

MIRABEAU PRESS

Published by Mirabeau Press

PO Box 4281

West Palm Beach, FL 33401

ISBN: 978-1-7357055-9-0

First Edition

MIRABEAU

I labour by singing light
Not for ambition or bread
Or the strut and trade of charms
On the ivory stages
But for the common wages
Of their most secret heart.

In My Craft or Sullen Art, Dylan Thomas

Once again, I have no general theory of anything to impart. Is this wisdom, laziness, or both?

In a castle in Scotland, now a hotel, I found in its library the first volume of the Reverend Hugh Blair's *Sermons*. It was of the fifteenth edition, having been first published twenty years earlier. At one time I should have despised such literature, but now I no longer do so and even read it (within limits) for pleasure, though I have not in the meantime become in the slightest religious. Eighteenth century sermons are full of sound sense, though of course one does not want to read hundreds of pages of sound sense at a sitting, even if one agrees with most of it. One does not read only to confirm what one already thought or believed.

Hugh Blair (1718–1800) was one of the most popular preachers of his day and, as the number of editions of his sermons testifies, his wisdom was much admired. He was Professor of Rhetoric and Belles Lettres at Edinburgh University and, apparently, an important theorist of rhetoric. He was no religious fanatic, and counted David Hume, an atheist philosopher if ever there was one, among his friends.

I turned to the eighth sermon in the book, with the title *On the Ignorance of Good and Evil in This Life*. The Eighteenth Century was an age of elegance in dress, furniture, silver, architecture, and so forth, but also in prose: and perhaps in mind as well, for it is not easy to write elegantly if you do not think clearly (though no doubt there is an elegant way to say nothing, or nothing much). The relation of elegance to truth is uncertain, for you can be clear of mind and deeply mistaken at the same time.

Blair begins his sermon eloquently:

The measure according to which knowledge is disposed

3

to man affords conspicuous proofs of divine wisdom. In many instances we clearly perceive, that either more or less would have proved detrimental to his state; that entire ignorance would have deprived him of proper motives to action; and that complete discovery would have raised him to a sphere too high for his present powers.

Our knowledge increases but our ignorance remains infinite. Unfortunately, even our partial knowledge has sometimes 'raised us to a sphere too high for our present powers'. It is commonly remarked, and has become a cliché, that technical prowess has not resulted in greater wisdom, and Blair means 'by his present powers' Man's ability to know, or to pursue, what is good for him.

He quotes Solomon, the sceptic, who asks 'Who knoweth what is good for man in this life?' He, Blair, continues:

> The whole history of mankind forms a comment on the doctrine of the Text. When we review the course of human affairs, one of the first objects which everywhere attracts our notice, is the mistaken judgment of men concerning their own interest.

You can say that again! But Blair is of the same opinion as Doctor Johnson, that dissatisfaction is the permanent condition of mankind:

> Around us, we everywhere behold a busy multitude. Restless and uneasy in their present situation, they are

incessantly employed in accomplishing a change of it; and as soon as their wish is fulfilled, we discern, by their behaviour, that they are as dissatisfied as they were before. Where they expected to have found a paradise, they found a desert. The man of business pines for leisure. The leisure for which he has longed proves an irksome gloom; and, through want of employment, he languishes, sickens, and dies. The man of retirement fancies no state is so happy, as that of an active life. But he has not engaged long in the tumults and contests of the world, until he finds cause to look back with regret on the calm hours of his former privacy and retreat. Beauty, wit, eloquence, and fame, are equally desired by persons in every rank of life... yet in what unnumbered instances have they proved, to those that possessed them, no other than shining snares; seductions to vice, instigations to folly, and in the end, sources of misery?

What is Blair's solution to this problem (he overlooks the possibility that some people who are beautiful, intelligent, eloquent and famous might actually be happy, or at any rate happier than those who are none of those things)?

God hath appointed out situation to be so ambiguous, in order both to call forth the exertion of those intelligent powers which he hath given us, and to enforce our dependence on his gracious aid.

This leads him (Blair) to conclude:

Let our ignorance of good and evil determine us to follow Providence, and to resign ourselves to God. One of the most important lessons which can be given to man, is resignation to his Maker.

We should therefore follow God's word and God's wishes: but this naturally brings us to the question of what God's wishes are and how we may know them? On this rather important subject, Blair, at least in this sermon, remains silent. I was rather reminded of the advice I gave my patients, that they did not need so much to find themselves as to lose themselves. When they asked how they were to lose themselves, I replied that it should be by being interested in something other than, or outside, themselves. 'And how do I do that?' they would ask, quite logically, and it was here that my system fell apart, for I could provide no definitive answer. Perhaps an activity might come first and then an interest in it develop afterwards, as it is sometimes said that addressing yourself to God leads to faith rather than the other way round.

In the castle-hotel, I read another sermon, number XII, on the duties and consolations of the aged. One passage particularly struck me, now that I must count myself as among the aged:

Though the querulous temper imparted to old age, is to be considered a natural infirmity, rather than as a vice; the same apology cannot be made for that peevish disgust at the manners, and the malignant censure of the enjoyments, of the young, which is sometimes found to accompany declining years.

What, I thought, I peevish? How dare Blair suggest it! All my disgust at the manners and enjoyments of the young of today is fully justified and the natural conclusion of close and objective observation. Just look around you! I was speaking to a Norwegian teacher in his early thirties the other day and he said exactly the same: and by no stretch of the imagination could he have been called old. Blair continues:

> It is too common to find the aged at declared enmity with the whole system of present customs and manners; perpetually complaining of the growing depravity of the world, and of the astonishing vices and follies of the rising generation. All things, according to them, are rushing fast into ruin... Similar lamentations were, in the day of your youth, poured forth by your fathers... Great has been the corruption of the world in every age.

The difference is that, *this* time, it is all true.

Edinburgh, compared with the last time I was there, ten years earlier, appalled me. It was not the criminal architecture approved by the no doubt corrupt city council that appalled me most, disgraceful as it was, as much as the dirt, the use of alleyways as public lavatories, the uncollected litter, and the depredations of the cheap commercialism consequent upon mass tourism, to say nothing of the constant stream in the streets of the seemingly gormless in both directions, like the crowds leaving a football match. Humanity in the mass is not attractive, at least to me.

I went to a second-hand bookshop that I had visited ten years before. I suppose it was a triumph that it had survived at all, but it had deteriorated, not only in the quality of its stock, but in the loud rock music that the owner, or manager, thought it was right to pump through the shop like poison gas. Did he not realise that bookish browsers need silence, that most precious of commodities, in order to be able to concentrate? I descended into the basement to escape the music, but it was there too, as inescapable as the speeches of the Great Leader in North Korea when I visited. Was this a sign of market failure or of a change in the market? I recalled a conversation I had some years ago with the owner of another bookshop who also played rock music loudly.

'You know,' I said, 'people who buy books want to browse in silence.'

'It's all right for you,' came the reply, 'but I'm here all day.'

That certainly put me in my place as a mere customer.

The idea that someone wanted to listen to, or at least hear, rock music all day as an antidote to terrifying silence appalled me.

Next to the bookshop, which I quickly fled, was a bric-a-brac establishment that largely sold costume jewellery to the type of person who needed external signs to express his or her individuality (there seems to have been a mass Edith-Sitwellisation of the population in this respect). There were a couple of shelves of books in the shop and among them was a slender volume in card covers published in 1940, a book, or booklet, of fifty poems by Robert Graves. It had an interesting inscription in pencil:

For Mary, With love from [name illegible]. 5.12.41.
Duplicate? Welcome? Hope so.

To this, in a different hand, a single word had been
appended:

Sure!

How good a poet was Graves? Insofar as he is widely
remembered at all, it is more for his war memoir, *Goodbye to All
That*, and his historical novels, *I, Claudius* and *Claudius the God*,
than for his poetry (he also wrote a novel about the Prince of
Poisoners, William Palmer, *They Hanged My Saintly Billy*, the
title supposedly being the words of Palmer's mother after his
execution). I doubt if many people know any of his poems by
heart, or even a single line of them.

Still, I found quite a few poems in this little book that I
thought powerful and moving. Published at the beginning of
the Second World War, the First was evidently still much on
his mind. This is hardly surprising. It is surely a very shallow
notion of the possibilities of human experience to believe that
there is some psychological technique that will enable a person
to put his memories, no matter of what degree of catastrophe,
behind him, as if they were merely official documents that
could be filed away and forgotten.

Repression of memory means more than one thing. It can
be a deliberate decision to put something into the back of one's
mind because one realises that to have it always at the
forefront is worse than useless, it is harmful. The memory has
not disappeared, however: it can be brought to the forefront

of the mind at will and may sometimes arrive unbidden.

Then there is the kind of repression beloved of psychotherapists, namely that of traumatic memories not available immediately to consciousness until a psychotherapist reveals them by his supposedly skilled procedures. Their recovery is supposed to be good for the patient. Whether this kind of repression actually exists is a matter of contention and I rather doubt it. Belief in it exists, but that is another matter.

Then there are the memories which come to mind when a stimulus brings them there. Graves' poem, *Recalling War*, begins:

> Entrance and exit wounds are silvered clean,
> The track aches only when the rain reminds.[1]

Everything is forgotten in the sense that nothing remains at the forefront of the mind forever:

> The one-legged man forgets his leg of wood,
> The one-armed man his jointed wooden arm.
> The blinded man sees with his ears and hands
> As much or more than once with both his ears.

Does this mean that mutilation does not matter, or that amnesia and adaptation will always compensate for or eliminate suffering, that hence in the long run nothing is of any account? Surely not: war is terrible. 'What, then, was

---

[1] This clearly refers to bullet wounds, with silver nitrate being used as an antiseptic.

war?' asks the first line of the second stanza of *Recalling War*.

> Natural infirmities were out of mode,
> For Death was young again: patron alone
> Of healthy dying, premature fate-spasm.

It was the young and healthy who died—were killed—in the war. Graves wrote his poem twenty years after the end of the war:

> And we recall the merry ways of guns –
> Nibbling the walls of factory and church
> Like a child, piecrust; felling groves of trees
> Like a child, dandelions with a switch.

These, surely, are fine images, making experiences that we have not had ourselves wonderfully (and horribly) clear to us. There is an infinity of despair, to which the author has a right, in the concluding lines:

> Machine-guns rattle toy-like from a hill,
> Down in a row the brave tin-soldiers fall;
> A sight to be recalled in elder days
> When learnedly the future we devote
> To yet more boastful vision of despair.

Strangely enough, this evocation of justified despair does not depress, it consoles us, why I cannot say. This is the greatest power of art, that it reconciles us to the suffering that is never far below the surface of human life.

Death—the lack of immortality—has always been a subject inspiring to poetry. Graves has a fine poem on death:

> To bring the dead to life
> Is no great magic.
> Few are wholly dead:
> Blow on a dead man's embers
> And a live flame will start.

This is true, of course, only while there is someone alive to blow on those embers. If you remember him:

> Assemble tokens intimate of him –
> A ring, a purse, a chair:
> Around these elements then build
> A home familiar to
> The greedy revenant.
> However, death cannot really be treated:
> So grant him life, but reckon
> That the grave which housed him
> May not be empty now.
> You in his spotted garments
> Shall yourself be wrapped.

This is not an original thought, but it is good poetry.

It cannot be easy to bear a name like von Schirach. Baldur of that name was one of the worst of the worst of the Nazis, a true believer in genocide, and he was lucky to escape hanging as others of his ilk were hanged. He was sentenced to twenty years' imprisonment and did not survive his release very long.

He was sixty-seven when he died.

His grandson, Ferdinand, has succeeded triumphantly in overcoming any legacy of that name. (If I had inherited it, I would have taken the easy path and changed it.) He has become among the best-known contemporary German writers worldwide.

He has been a defence advocate in serious criminal cases for many years, and his books evoke with great clarity the ambiguities inscribed in his cases. I suppose that the overall message of his books is 'There but for the grace of God go I,' though with the God left out. The difference between innocence and guilt is far from as clear as we like to think that it is. This is a message with which I am only in partial agreement: there are some cases in which guilt is so great as to be categorically distinct and different from innocence. To this, Schirach might reply, 'Ah, if only you knew *all* the circumstances.'

Would he apply that reasoning to his grandfather?

In any case, he is an excellent writer, again dispelling the idea, or suspicion, as Stefan Zweig did before him, that the German language is somehow inimical to clear writing, and intrinsically liable to verbose mystification. Whether or not one agrees with his basic outlook, his stories never fail to provoke thought and to move. His books deserved to be the best-sellers that they are—I make here a categorical judgment.

I read his last book in French, *Café et cigarettes*. It is a collection of short essays, almost like this book, except that it is not books that are the subject or occasion of the essays, but episodes or events in real life. In one of these essays, he uses, in my view incorrectly, Heisenberg's Uncertainty Principle.

He uses it to cast doubt on the possibility of real and final knowledge of events in the macroscopic world. Does that mean that we can never say that an event truly and definitely took place?

I don't want to carp. The book, made up of fragments, has a cumulative effect. There are stories that make us reverse our judgment of the character described. This reversal is an education in itself.

As I have mentioned before, one of the few consolations of growing old is the ease with which memories are evoked, the mind being so well-stored, and recollection, provided it is of something not too painful, is a pleasure in itself. Many things come to act as the madeleine in Proust.

The tenth of the forty-eight chapters (in a book only 160 pages long) evoked memories in me that were happy because amusing, to me at least. It recounts the time the editor of a 'lifestyle' magazine asked Schirach to attend and report on Paris Fashion Week, although he had no knowledge of or interest in fashion.

This was very curious to me because an English newspaper once asked me to do precisely the same at London Fashion Week, though I was as ignorant and uninterested as Schirach.

Our experiences were in many respects identical. We were both struck by the artificiality, the superficiality, frivolity, insincerity and hypocrisy of this world. The models upon whom the clothes of the couturiers were draped were of the same kind. In Schirach:

> The mannequins make their appearance, their faces are made up in dark tints, one would think them the Erinyes,

the Greek goddesses of vengeance. None of them smiled...The young women have an extremely troubled look, with stick-silhouettes without breasts or buttocks... A little later, somebody explained to me that the mannequins fed themselves exclusively on ice cubes and cotton that they dipped in orange juice.

This was precisely what I saw myself, and later read in the memoir of a French mannequin who escaped that evil world and became, or trained to be, an actress. Of course, she had chosen the life for herself, against the wishes of her parents, out of an attraction to its cheap glamour; nevertheless, by the end of her book, which I believed to be a true account, I came to think that the correct place for couturiers, at least of the London and Paris fashion week variety, is prison. No slave owner was ever more exploitative than they.

Curiously enough, I met a German fashion photographer at London Fashion Week. She asked me whether I was a fashion journalist.

'No,' I replied. 'I know nothing about fashion and have no interest in it.'

'And yet you are writing an article about it?' she asked, incredulously.

'Yes,' I said. 'Don't you see, that's the whole point?'

'In Germany,' she said in a tone of national superiority, 'this would not be possible.'

By contrast, I thought that it was a sign of national superiority because in Britain it *was* possible. But we were both wrong, because Schirach was about to do precisely the same for a German publication. Is it possible that the German editor who commissioned the article was inspired by my own article? Or perhaps the other way round? The latter is less likely because fewer English editors read German than German editors read English: but as Heisenberg might have put it, one never knows.

One of my enduring memories of London Fashion Week was the announcement that this year's colours (I forget which year it was) were 'trashy'. This was the first time I had heard the word 'trashy' used in any sense other than derogatory. It seemed to imply a largeness of mind that saw worth in the trashy. This frivolity appalled me: the world has enough ugliness in it already without straining after it to increase it. One of the exhibitors at the Fashion Week was the late Vivienne Westwood. After her death, praise of her in the public media was loud and unanimous. I know nothing of her as a person—perhaps she was the soul of kindliness, the treatment of the mannequins notwithstanding—but it seemed to me, and still seems to me, that she left the world a little uglier than she found it, and her relation to beauty was that of Satanists to the ceremony of the Mass.

Surely one of the most extraordinary of all golden ages in human history is that of Dutch art in the seventeenth century. Even the firmest disbeliever in the concept of golden ages must concede that this was one. But just as extraordinary, in a way, was its abrupt end. No doubt there were competent Dutch artists in the eighteenth century who could turn out the likeness of a man in a velvet or brocade coat, and of a woman in silk or satin, but even those who could, without difficulty, name thirty or forty Dutch artists of the seventeenth century would be hard put to name even one of the eighteenth.

What was the cause of this very sudden decline, this effervescence in reverse? I have asked many people, educated but not art historians, and it was clear that they had never given a moment's thought to this strange phenomenon; but once they did, they came up with an obvious but unsatisfactory answer, indicative of our tendency to ascribe overwhelming importance to economic factors in life. The Dutch economy declined, and therefore its art too: such was the answer given. But economic predominance is neither a necessary nor a sufficient condition for the production of great art, so much is clear, though I have no better explanation to offer. The fact that you can't explain something yourself is, however, no reason to accept someone else's inadequate explanation of it.

In 1954, the art historian who made a fortune from his attribution of paintings to famous Italian artists of past centuries, Bernard Berenson, published a little book titled *The Arch of Constantine, or the Decline of Form.* In this essay, he examines the sculpture on the Arch of Constantine, the triumphal arch built in AD 312 to honour the victory of the Emperor Constantine over the Emperor Maxentius at the Battle of the Milvian Bridge. If the battle had gone the other way, no doubt there would have been an Arch of Maxentius for Berenson to have dilated upon.

But if Berenson is right, its sculpted elements would have been just as inferior to previous models as those of the Arch of Constantine. By a close examination of these, Berenson shows, admittedly in a slightly contrived way, that the art of sculpture in Rome had declined precipitously in quality for the previous two or three decades, such that the sculptural elements on the Arch were crude, unlifelike and degenerate in comparison with what had been done not so very long before.

Of course, the idea that there has been a decline requires that there is a standard by which works of art are to be judged as superior. No doubt there are some who deny that there is, or ever could be, such a standard, because *de gustibus*, etc. It is true that it is difficult to prove the existence of such a standard from a metaphysical Archimedean point: nor is there a metre rule somewhere that guarantees its objectivity. But yet I think that no one really believes this in his heart, so that when he says that Mozart is superior to rap music he is merely stating a personal preference, in effect only that 'I prefer Mozart.' While on the one hand we cannot justify judgment, on the other we cannot do without it.

On the subject of Berenson's financial honesty there is more than one opinion, but there is no doubt that he was a clever and learned man, and it was a clever strategy of his argument to take the sculptures of the Arch of Constantine and to compare them with work completed by the same civilisation only shortly before. Half of this slim volume is taken up with black and white photographs, one picture, or in this context *two* pictures, being worth more, far more, than a thousand words. And looking at the photographs of the work done before the Arch was built, and the work on the Arch, I think there can be little doubt that the latter was much cruder and less refined than the former.

Berenson will have nothing to do with the argument that

the new crudity was simply a new form of artistic expression. On the contrary, he believes it to be the consequence of the loss of artistic ability to be found in the city. Its able artists had fled towards the east. The artistic as well as the political gravity of the Empire was moving eastwards. (The defeated Emperor, Maxentius, was the last to make Rome his capital and to have lived there throughout his reign.) All who were left in Rome were mere craftsmen who had only a vague idea of how the artists had designed and made their sculptures. They copied them, but not very successfully, for the kind of skill necessary to produce work of that quality was not to be acquired quickly but was a) the fruit of a long tradition and b) required the lifelong training that could not simply be willed into existence.

Berenson argued that it was inconceivable that the city of Rome did not employ the best sculptors available to it for a work such as the Arch of Constantine, and therefore that the sculpture on the Arch really did represent a decline. Perhaps a doctor influenced by the concept of *evidence-based medicine* might demand further evidence that the decline was general and not just evident on one edifice, requiring random samples of sculpture from before and during the erection of the Arch to make a proper comparison. Still, it seems plausible that the best possible craftsmen, artisans and artists would have worked on so important a commission. Constantine, after all, was not just *any* old emperor.

You might suppose that the whole argument was an arcane, antiquarian one, but not a bit of it. Berenson was using it as a stalking horse for what he saw as the decline of western art in the previous half century. The technical capacity of artists (so he argued) was in steepening decline and this could be seen in their figuration, clearly crude in the same way as the figuration on the Arch of Constantine was crude. Importantly, he denies that the crudity of the latter was a search for a different, expressionistic way of depicting humans: incompetence was the explanation.

I will quote a passage in the book that sums up what many feel, perhaps too sweepingly, has gone wrong with modern western art:

> Periodically there come moments when the problems, ideas, and interests that have been inspiring and guiding artists, are played out, either owing to altered conditions which entail loss of interest in their style, or because of demands which they are not prepared to meet, and leave the artists not knowing what to do. They search and chip and daub and smear with a vague urge, perhaps, but no pattern in their minds. Accidentally, the less incompetent among them, those that have some natural endowment for their craft, produces something that satisfies their own conceit. They communicate this satisfaction to their literary friends and these seldom fail to persuade the craftsman that his craving or painting is an example of carefully thought-out, purposeful, metaphysically grounded, priceless newness.

All that is solid melts into the air, said Marx of the constant change wrought by the capitalist bourgeoisie in constant search for a new source of profit. And true it is that all that we had supposed immutable, that we thought rested on a solid foundation, may collapse, fade away, disappear in a comparative instant. I write this at a time when the world, which seemed tolerably stable only a short time ago (which is not the same a happy, I hasten to add) now trembles on the verge of several possible, even likely, catastrophes.

I recently read two very disparate books in succession: but yet there was something important that they had in common. The first was a novel by Hugh Walpole, titled *The Secret City*, and the second a memoir by Benjamin Stora, the French historian, titled *L'Arivée*, The Arrival.

Walpole, who died in 1941, was a fashionable and successful novelist of whom Somerset Maugham wrote slightingly in his novel, *Cakes and Ale*. (I read Walpole's book because I wanted to know why Maugham should have launched so hurtful an attack on a man who had counted him as his friend and who, whatever his faults, was not so bad a man that he deserved a vicious attack both on his work and his character.)

Walpole spent several years in Russia and wrote two novels based on his experience. He acted as a medical assistant on the Eastern Front during the First World War, and he described this in *The Dark Forest*, published in 1916. The outcome of the war—if it can be said to have had a single outcome—was thus still unknown. Walpole seems to me to lack the ruthlessness of the true writer: he only hints at the horrors he has seen, not because what is said indirectly is more effective than what is said directly, but to spare the readers' feelings. Of course, he was working under wartime restrictions; complete frankness would have had to wait until the war was over. Nevertheless, one has the suspicion that it was not censorship that deterred him from writing in an unvarnished fashion about what he had seen: he was more interested in the ups and downs of the emotional lives of his characters than in the slaughter of millions.

The Secret City was published in 1919, two years after the Bolshevik coup d'état. It recounts the story of the Markovitch family in Petrograd, in the months before the February Revolution of 1917, and the months following it, whom the narrator, clearly the writer himself, frequented.

The Markovitches are members of the bourgeois intelligentsia, almost bohemians, and what is most striking about them is that they have no inkling of the catastrophe which is soon to engulf them. On the very eve of the Revolution, their preoccupation is to go to the theatre to see Meyerhold's spectacular new production. It seemed to them of the greatest importance, far greater than that of the Revolution itself.

We know Meyerhold's fate as Walpole did not when he wrote his book. Meyerhold's wife was murdered in their flat in 1939 by the security forces, and Meyerhold himself was arrested, severely tortured and shot by firing squad in 1940. And he, be it remembered, had been favourably disposed towards the Bolsheviks!

The insouciance of the Markovitch family, the scale of which even the author himself could have had no idea, was what I most remember of the book. They were dancing on the edge of a volcano without knowing it. To the very end, they were more concerned with their emotional lives than with public affairs—those public affairs of which Doctor Johnson said, mistakenly, that they 'vexed no man'. Happy are those who live in an epoch when Doctor Johnson was right (if such an epoch has ever existed)! The problem is that, while you may not be interested in politics, politics is interested in you— or at least will affect you.

Benjamin Stora's *L'Arivée* is his account of, and reflections on, his departure from Constantine in Algeria in 1962. Jews had lived there for two millennia, and Stora grew up speaking Arabic at home. Because his father was well-liked in the city and knew some of the Algerian leaders personally, he was very late to make arrangements to leave after independence. He, like many others, mistook the nature of the Algerian Revolution, thinking it more secular than it was.

Leaving it so late to flee, Stora's father was able to take only what he could carry when he and his family left for France. The Storas had nothing to show for the untold generations who had lived in Constantine. Stora *père*, like the Markovitches, did not realise that he had been dancing on the edge of a volcano. He had assumed that, notwithstanding the disturbances, life would continue more or less as it always had—'always' meaning within living memory.

How could this not remind me of my own family history, albeit that I know of it in very little detail, for it was never spoken of. My mother, aged 19, arrived in England from Nazi Germany in January, 1939, with practically no memento of her previous life as the daughter of a bourgeois Jewish family in Berlin. Her father was a doctor who had been a major in the Imperial German Army in the First World War, winning the Iron Cross. No doubt he believed that his beloved Germany could not remain Nazi for very long, and indeed as a veteran was probably spared for a time the worst effects of early Nazi rule. According to letters in my possession, he continued to practise as a doctor even after the passage of the Nuremberg Laws, though whether he still had any gentile patients I do not know. At any rate, his life as a comfortable bourgeois, complete with expensive chauffeur-driven cars, seems to have continued. Presumably he hoped (and thought) that the storm would pass, and by the time he realised that it would not, it was too late. He, his wife, and my mother's older sister managed to get out to China in June, 1939, China being the only country that would accept them (they had even tried Haiti). My mother never saw them again. Both my grandparents died, almost at the same time, in Shanghai in 1944, in circumstances and conditions that I do not know. My grandparents' German citizenship was restored to them in 1952, eight years after their death.

Benjamin Stora writes of the silence about the Algerian years that prevailed in his family after its removal to France— precisely my mother's silence about her German years until she died aged 85. I always instinctively understood that her silence was the way in which she overcame a pain too deep to be repaired by words. I regret that my mother's experience died with her, but my curiosity was essentially idle or prurient, so different, and easier, had been my own passage through life.

The effect of reading these two books in quick succession was not entirely reassuring. Are we not all, always, dancing on the edge of a volcano, and will not our successors marvel at how blind to the obvious we were? Luckily, I am of an age at which the future is not of great importance to me, only the past. But I pity the generations to come.

No one who visited Albania during the communist epoch is likely to forget the experience. It made other communist countries (except North Korea) seem like havens of freedom. It elevated paranoia into the fundamental principle of the state.

It is very odd, however, that from this most total of totalitarian countries (except North Korea) should have emerged, or been allowed to emerge, a great writer, Ismail Kadare. I have long wondered what his relations with the little Stalin of Albania, Enver Hoxha, were, or what horrible compromises he must have made, in order to be published at all. He must have skated on very thin ice or, to change the metaphor, walked a very narrow and twisting path. I don't suppose the truth will be told until after his death, if then.[2]

Reading his latest book (he is now, as I write this, eighty-seven years old), *The Dictator Calls*, is surely indirectly a meditation on his own condition as a writer under a totalitarian dictatorship. He does not tell us how close the analogies were between his case and that of Boris Pasternak, but he certainly implies that there were many. For example, Kadare has been nominated for the Nobel Prize (which he has so far not received, though he is many times more worthy of it than, say, Bob Dylan), a prize that Pasternak was awarded though he was not permitted to receive it. The award did not improve Pasternak's life: according to Kadare, citing others, it

---

[2] He died shortly after this had been written but not yet published.

may actually have killed him.

In 1934, Pasternak received a telephone call from Stalin himself. Stalin asked Pasternak what he thought of Osip Mandelstam, who had just been arrested. Pasternak is supposed to have replied in a non-committal way, saying that Mandelstam's style was different from his own, he was of a different school of poetry, etc. Stalin is said to have replied that if he had been Mandelstam's friend (as he supposed Pasternak to have been), he would have known better how to defend him.

The effrontery of what Stalin said—if he did indeed say it—takes the breath away. To create conditions of generalised terror and then reproach people for being afraid takes some gall. No doubt it was especially delicious to Stalin to take his revenge in this way on a man when his own genius was only for intrigue and ruthlessness (though he had once been a poet in his native language, Georgian, and some of his poems appeared in pre-revolutionary anthologies of Georgian poetry). But he was far from an ignoramus or a philistine; it was perhaps a tribute to his powers of discrimination that he chose Pasternak to humiliate in this way. It was the compliment of a monster.

Is it possible that Hoxha once telephoned Kadare in the same fashion and asked him a similar question about an Albanian man of letters whom he had just had arrested and was preparing to kill? (Mandelstam was killed not after his first, but his second, arrest.) Certainly, Kadare left it very late in the day to seek asylum from Albania in France, in 1990, by which time it was obvious that the regime could not long survive. This was strange indeed. Was it because by then the regime had lost the courage of its brutality, and would not have dared, as it once would, to have persecuted the family of anyone claiming asylum? Or was it because he feared revelations of his compromises with Hoxha that had permitted him fame and a comfortable existence, while up to ten per cent of the population had been arrested in their lifetime, and the population was constantly obliged to celebrate its own enslavement in public? The desire for revenge, after all, was hardly alien to the Albanian mentality. I hope by this hypothesis that I am libelling him, as I might very well be. Let him who is without cowardice case the first stone; let him who has never lived under a totalitarian regime recall his own frailty.

The one thing that I shall always remember from this book when I have forgotten all else (which will be very quickly, my memory being poor), is the conversation Kadare describes from his time as a student in Moscow at the Gorky Institute in Khruschev's day. The institute was the most prestigious school of literature of the Soviet Union, and the conversation was with a Latvian student called Stolpens. The latter had seen the now-famous photograph of Lenin in his bath chair during his last illness, which made him look the very incarnation of demented evil. Kadare tells Stolpens that he is surprised that the photograph was allowed to survive, considering Lenin's god-like status under the Soviet regime.

Stolpens's reply is memorable. He says that Lenin's last illness—the final stages of syphilis—was the one human thing about him. It suggests that he once resorted to a prostitute, which was possibly the only human thing this inhuman man ever did. In other words, he was so evil a man that something that would have been discreditable in anyone else was comparatively good in him.

Pictures of Lenin's brain post-mortem that I have seen, if genuine, indicate a degree of atrophy that I have hardly seen equalled. Clearly, such atrophy was not the work of a moment, but of a long process. It suggests that you don't need much of a brain to rule after a vast country, if you order enough executions. What part such atrophy played in Lenin's total inhumanity no one will ever know. His ideology was always lacking in real sympathy for actual human beings and if ever he felt any stirrings of such feelings he immediately suppressed them as inhibitory of what he thought it necessary to do, which was to murder hundreds of thousands, or millions. Famously, he said that when he listened to the *Pathétique* sonata, he wanted to pat the heads of children—so no more Beethoven for him.[3]

On this subject of syphilis in its last stages, I believe that Nietzsche's grandiosity was attributable to it, a pathetic little mouse of a man claiming in his circumstances of total insignificance to be the most dangerous person who ever lived. Such grandiosity contrasting with a person's actual situation is, according to Brain's *Clinical Neurology* (4th Edition, 1951), characteristic of General Paralysis of the Insane (GPI) before the patient declines into terminal amentia, the absence of all mental activity whatever, which fits precisely with Nietzsche's case. Lenin also declined into amentia, alas far too late.

It is surely curious for me to read as much as I do but to

---

[3] Stalin loved Mozart.

retain so little. Perhaps it is as well not to clutter one's mind too much. The Soviet psychologist, A.R. Luria, wrote a book, *The Mind of a Mnemonist*, about a man who could forget nothing and who therefore led a wretched life. Perhaps it is as well to read a whole book, even as short a one as *A Dictator Calls*, and remember only one thing: that Lenin's syphilis was the one human thing about him. That, at least, is an arresting thought.

On a train from London to Paris, I decided to re-read *The Tempest*. I bought an edition at the surprisingly excellent bookshop in St Pancras station. You can tell something about the passengers who use a station by the books on sale in it: the bookshop in the Gare de Lyon is as superior to that in the Gare du Nord as is that of St Pancras to that of Euston. In the latter, I once counted seven titles with the word *Fuck* in them. I dare not say *what* it is that you can conclude from such differences, so incendiary might the conclusion be.

I am not one of those who can cite from memory whole pages of Shakespeare, and though I have read many of the plays several times, when I re-read them I always discover that I have forgotten much. I also discover things that I do not think that I saw in them before, though maybe I did and have simply forgotten them. I am an allusive reader, which is to say that I find things in a play that remind me of something in my own life, or of some aspect of the world around me. And so it was on the train with *The Tempest*, which I was reading for the nth time.

I had recently been reading about Derek Parfit, the

philosopher, whom several philosophers have called great, but who seems to me to make extremely heavy weather of establishing philosophically that the pursuit of self-interest cannot be the best policy and that it would be self-contradictory to take it as such. It was of him that I thought when, on board the ship in the storm that is to land the party of Antonio, Sebastian etc. on Prospero's island, Gonzalo says to the boatswain, 'Yet remember whom thou has aboard.' The Boatswain replies, 'None that I love more than myself.'

In other words, because of self-love or self-interest, he is bound to do his best; and yet we know, or think that we do, that crews of ships ensure the safety of passengers before their own, and indeed are shocked if they do not: if instead of being the last to abandon ship, they are the first. Whether this was the morality of ships' crews in Shakespeare's day, I do not know; when it first developed would be an interesting historical question. The notes to the edition that I bought said nothing on this point. (I should add that it was sold me by a very tall half-caste woman with splendid tresses and superior diction, who told me that she had played Miranda in her school production of the play. O, brave new world that has such people in it!)

Gonzalo goes on to say that he has great confidence in the boatswain because 'He hath no drowning mark upon him. His complexion is perfect yellow.' This derives from the proverb that 'He that is born to be hanged shall never be drowned'. But is anyone born to be hanged? This is a very complex question, as is the relation of a person's physiognomy to his character.

Can a person be born to be hanged? A congenital fate can

be congenital either genetically or environmentally, or more usually some combination of the two. A tendency to break the accepted rules of society may be genetic in origin, but whether it is expressed will depend on many things in the environment. Thus, genetics may explain (to an extent) why person A rather than person B committed a crime, but not why criminality itself has increased, or decreased, generally. And one cannot be born to the gallows where there are no gallows to be born to.

Can a complexion be 'perfect gallows', as Gonzalo says of the boatswains? The Italian doctor, anthropologist and criminologist, Cesare Lombroso, thought so: that there were physical stigmata of criminality. This, of course, carries the implication that criminality is a kind of disease, though one without a cure, the search for which might entail many cruel absurdities. The best that could be hoped for on this view would be containment and, insofar as the illness was hereditary, eugenic control of reproduction.

Is there no art to find the mind's construction in the face, as Shakespeare puts it elsewhere? The fact is that, theoretical and empirical refutations of Lombroso aside, we are all Gonzalos when we encounter people for the first time. While we cannot say with Gwendolyn in *The Importance of Being Ernest* that our first impressions are never wrong, we cannot avoid having them, and they are often difficult to override in the face of evidence to the contrary. Therefore, what Gonzalo says is only what we all might say about the villainy proclaimed on a visage.

A little further in the play, as the ship is believed by everyone to be breaking up, voices of sailors offstage are heard

31

to cry 'We split, we split! Farewell my wife and children! Farewell, brother! We split, we split, we split!' Few of us now, I think, could hear this without recalling the telephone messages home of people caught in the World Trade Center in 2001, or in the aircraft that the hijackers intended to crash into the Pentagon, but which the passengers diverted to crash elsewhere.

In the next scene, Prospero says to his daughter Miranda, with whom he took refuge on the island when she was three years old:

> I have done nothing but in care of thee.
> Of thee, my dear one, thee, my daughter, who
> Art ignorant of what thou art, naught knowing
> Of whence I am, nor that I am more better
> Than Prospero, master of a poor fool cell,
> And thy no greater father.

To which Miranda replies, 'More to know/ Did never meddle with my thoughts.'

Here I thought of two adopted children whom I know, one my own age and one in her mid-twenties. In both cases, the adoption was entirely happy and in neither case did he or she to seek to meddle more to know. I thought it better thus and have always been sceptical of the benefits of the supposed rights of adopted children to meddle more to know: to meet their biological parents, or even to know that they were adopted. Some things are better swept under the carpet and kept there.

Prospero nevertheless tells her of her royal background and

Miranda says that she remembers:

> ... rather like a dream than an assurance...
> Had I not
> Four of five women once that tended me?

Prospero asks 'But how is it/ That this lives in thy mind? What seest thou else/ In the dark and backward abysm of time?'

Miranda remembers nothing else; and in this little passage Shakespeare captures perfectly the arbitrary or chance nature of early memories.

As it happens, I was also reading at the time the memoir of Frances Pitt titled *Country Days*. I was to give a lecture about her soon afterwards to the Bridgnorth Historical Society, the one assembly known to me in which my presence lowers the average age. Frances Pitt (1888-1964) lived near Bridgnorth, and in the 1920s, to the 1950s was one of the best-known nature writers in Britain. Her memoir, published in 1961, begins by remarking on the fact that her first memory, aged about 3, is of strawberries and that, like Miranda, she remembers nothing else of that time of her life. She says that early memories are laid down arbitrarily, without connection to importance (the Freudians, of course, then still in intellectual ascendence, would have disagreed).

I could—but won't—write an entire book about the mental associations and reflections that I had when reading *The Tempest* on the train to Paris. Wealth of association is one of the rewards of a long life.

Charles Morgan is an author who has something in common with Walter Scott: not his style or his subject matter, but the fact is that his books are usually to be found mouldering on the shelves of second-hand bookshops, such as still exist. He was once a fashionable author, more in France and the United States than in his native Britain, but after his death in 1958, and the cultural changes wrought in the 1960s, he fell out of fashion: hence his presence wherever second-hand books are sold.

Is this oblivion unjust, or at any rate does it deprive us of something of value? (There *is* a Charles Morgan society or fellowship, and a study of his novels was published in 2018, so oblivion is perhaps too strong a word.) But he is certainly not attuned to modern sensibility, though this is not necessarily a damning criticism. He disliked irony or facetiousness—which are not at all the same—and he seems to me to have eschewed humour altogether as being incompatible with seriousness: a grave misunderstanding and, one might almost say, character defect. Pictures of him on the internet show him to have been rather severe of aspect; I think I should have been rather intimidated by him if I had met him and am rather glad I did not. He looked a little like Christopher Lee in his role as Dracula (how I loved those films as an adolescent!). Morgan was self-consciously a stylist, the kind of man who would go to lengths not to end a sentence with a preposition. I approve of good style, of course, but not when it becomes too self-conscious or mannered, almost a reproach to the reader, as if it were a pearl cast before swine. It seems to imply that 'You are not worthy of me,' in much the same way as a waiter in an expensive restaurant tells the customers how the vegetables were raised and then picked before noon or after sunset, or some such.

It was not only his style that was fastidious, everything about him seemed to have been fastidious. His mode of dress was quietly elegant, in a way that has now almost departed from this world. Even his manner of holding a cigarette was fastidious, though no doubt his stale cigarette ash smelt as badly as anyone else's (even if his cigarettes were of a superior Balkan or Turkish variety). In those days, no one would have noticed the smell imparted to his clothes because in those days three quarters of men, and a half of women, smoked, and everything that could have absorbed the smell of smoke— curtains, tablecloths, upholstery—must have done so. It is strange how fastidiousness can change object: and now it is sufficient for me to pass someone smoking a cigarette in the street for me to start coughing and feel much put upon. I suspect that Morgan bought his cigarettes in Jermyn Street.

It is his thought and feeling that is most fastidious. The emotions and thoughts of his characters are so refined that it is sometimes difficult to know what they are. For some reason, he put me in mind of the late Francis King, another refined novelist, whom I once or twice met, or at least sat near, at luncheons at *The Spectator* (I don't think he ever had a mere lunch). I was neither sufficiently interesting nor refined to for him to talk to, and I remember him particularly for his finger movements, which were like the antennae of very nervous insects. His fingers would approach a physical object and then, quivering and agitated, not quite pick it up, as if materiality were in itself a little vulgar. Perhaps the object was not quite good enough for him, or disappointed him in some way.

I think Morgan might have been a little like that. He would have preferred a world made of the finest porcelain. Certainly, he was offended by the ugly and the gross; but even if the purely aesthetic approach to life can become tiresome, and is certainly not sufficient, I prefer it to its opposite, namely a preference for the ugly because beauty confronts us with our own nothingness. Besides, if much of the world is perforce ugly because we, mankind, have made it so, it requires a kind of lazy stoicism to accept it as such. Extreme aestheticism may not be the solution, but it is at least an implicit recognition that something is wrong.

Morgan, who had been in the navy and interned in Holland in the First World War, published his short novel, *The Empty Room*, in 1941. My copy, a third reprint that dates from 1944, is in perfect condition. At the time, Morgan must have been regarded almost as a national treasure, for the standard of production of his book was very high, much higher than that of most books produced in Britain today, or than that of books of other authors produced at the time, printed as it was on good thick paper and beautifully bound. Perhaps, though, it had something to do with the fact that in that year he also published a history of the publishing firm of Macmillan, his own publisher throughout his career.

To have set a novel in the early war years during the early war years themselves, as did Morgan, was certainly bold, for the outcome was then far from clear and not a foregone conclusion. But the war enters only tangentially into the real story, which however begins:

> On the last Saturday of November, the third month of
> the war, Richard Cannock performed, on a woman's eye,
> a bold and simple operation that gave him the
> satisfaction a writer may have in a flawless paragraph.

The imagined writer, one surmises, is Morgan himself,
contemplating a perfect paragraph about the pleasure of
contemplating a perfect paragraph.

Cannock is in the Garrick Club, lamenting the removal of
its paintings for safety's sake. The wine steward serves him a
pint of claret, that is to say something more than two thirds of
a bottle. It is lunchtime: one can only hope that he has no
operations to perform in the afternoon.

The next day, he goes to a research laboratory where, with
his knowledge of optics, he is to develop bombsights for
aircraft, and the like. He is forty-four years old but already
considers himself an elderly man. He lodges at the house of an
old friend called Rydal, a barrister-turned-legal historian. The
latter laments the passing of the limited state in favour of a
state responsible for everything. Rydal is writing a book whose
purpose is to show, less by argument than by objective history,
how far and by what stages a democratic people, under stress
of war and the pressure of bureaucracy, has moved from their
principles of freedom; how, in England, Parliament has
delegated to the Executive power to legislate by decree...

This was eighty years ago! But the book is not mainly
political: it is semi-mystical, and for my taste the writing is
somewhat flatulent, always straining at a meaning that it never
quite conveys. I will not rehearse the plot further, not so as not
to spoil it for future readers, whom I surmise will be few, but

because it is boring, oozing an attempted significance as a snail leaves a trail behind it. Curiously enough, the flap of the dust jacket quotes a review in the *Sunday Times* which seems less than laudatory:

> But there are some wise and lovely things in this book, which at least leaves the reader thinking hard.

I think if I had been in charge of the publisher's publicity department, I would have replaced the words 'But' and 'at least' by dishonest ellipses.

Interestingly, Morgan's book in 1944 cost in nominal terms one fifth of a single first-class postage stamp today, a powerful reminder of the degradation of the currency; but even now a first edition of many of Morgan's books are to be had for only sixty per cent of the said postage stamp, which is an implicit commentary on his current reputation and popularity.

I bought Heinrich Wiegand Petzet's *Le Chemin de l'étoile: Rencontre et causeries avec Heidegger* (translated from the original German into an English version as *Encounters and Dialogues with Martin Heidegger, 1929-1976)* because it was nicely printed and reduced in price from 24 to 8 euros. There was a sketch of Heidegger on the front cover that made him look like a lowly bank clerk who has got away with a vast scheme of embezzlement.

Heidegger is said by many to have been one of the most important philosophers of the twentieth century, and since

Raymond Tallis, the cleverest man I know, says so, I am prepared to believe it; by others, though, he is regarded as near to a fraud. He is certainly not easy to read and I have always given up after a few pages. What he writes is beyond me; therefore, I am completely unqualified to give an opinion on the still-burning question of whether there is any intrinsic connection between his philosophy and his Nazism. My fundamental stance in such matters is that two and two make four whoever, even the Devil himself, says it, so that if Heidegger's philosophy is of any value, insofar as it is not specifically *political* philosophy, it is of value whatever his political views or engagements.

The book I bought was by Heidegger's friend of fifty years, and whatever Heidegger's ambivalence about Nazism in the movement's early days (his waiting and seeing), the book offers insight into both the man and his times.

Heidegger was famous before the Nazis' arrival in power, and there seems to have been a cult that grew up around him. This might have been with his cooperation: no one becomes a guru without some acquiescence on his own part. Petzet writes of the time before 1933, when he himself was a student:

> Everyone was agreed in saying that, in his external appearance, Heidegger was already very different from how one imagined him. He had nothing of the intellectual: he had more the air of a peasant or a workman. But as soon as one saw his eyes, one was captivated by his way of looking, and we knew it could only be Heidegger. 'A seer, a thinker, who sees' (Gadamer)... For those who listened to him attentively,

the flow of his most difficult ideas became simple and intelligible. The high timbre of his voice, with that particular warmth of his classical German accent almost without variety, but without monotony, commanded extreme attention; his abandonment, evident in its intensity, to thought itself... all this contributed to the singular fascination of this man and what he said.

The fascination of the personage is the essence of gurudom, and I suppose may be exercised either voluntarily or involuntarily; but it seems to be inimical to the exercise of the critical judgment of others. No doubt it is also destructive of the critical faculties of the guru himself: no one feels himself as all-wise as he who is regarded as all-wise by others. The guru must take himself with deadly seriousness and he cannot treat of minor subjects or mundanities such as interest most people most of the time—questions such as whether or not Heidegger was a convinced Nazi, a subject of interest even to non-philosophers.

Another anecdote suggests that Heidegger consciously played the guru, though this does not affect the value or otherwise of his philosophy. Petzet arrived at Heidegger's house by appointment with some proofs for Heidegger to correct. Heidegger returned from a walk, having forgotten all about the rendezvous. He asked Petzet to wait, and then, half an hour later, called him into his study. He asked Petzet whether he could not return the following day, because then he would be able to talk for longer; on that day, he was on the way to an important thought and he couldn't let himself be distracted from its path. Petzet agreed, but just as he was leaving, Heidegger said that perhaps he could look at the proofs straight away, and that tomorrow he would be free to talk of something else more important philosophically than the correction of proofs.

Perhaps I am overinterpreting here, but I see insincerity in this, untruthfulness and an almost childish desire by Heidegger to impress by claiming the arduousness of his thought. Perhaps I have never thought arduously enough for this to seem real to me: I admit that my trains of thought tend to be short, locomotives not followed by many wagons or carriages. I can imagine an experimental scientist saying 'I have an experiment to complete,' or a writer saying, 'I want just to finish a paragraph' (I have said it many times myself), or a mathematician saying the he is just finishing—not correcting—a mathematical proof. But to me, there appears something exhibitionistic about Heidegger's conduct here (I assume Petzet accurately reports it). But even if I am right, the anecdote would go to defect of character, and not a very severe one, rather than to any weakness of his philosophy.

Recently, I happened to read the biographies of two English philosophers of very different stamp from Heidegger, J.L. Austin and Derek Parfit. Both, it seems to me, had something of the guru about them, and both became the objects of a cult following. Wittgenstein was definitely the founder of a cult, for his followers began to talk, dress and walk like him. One might have thought that people—philosophers—whose main ambition in life was to pursue truth would be resistant to the siren-song of discipleship, but it appears not. If anything, perhaps, they are more than usually prone to it...

Another anecdote does not reflect well on Heidegger,

though the author is barely 'this side idolatry'. For several years after the war, Heidegger was not allowed to teach. He was invited, however, to speak at the Munich Academy, on the subject of *the thing*. Near the time, he received a message seemingly to prescribe the style of his discourse, and Heidegger was so outraged that he cancelled the event for good. He was indignant that he should be dictated to in this fashion. 'Nothing similar happened to me in Hitler's time!' he said.

This suggests a profound moral and philosophical defect in a man who practically never said a word about the Holocaust. The prescription of the style of a single talk by him moved him far more than the deaths of millions. This was intellectual egotism, self-importance and even, on this occasion, stupidity that it would be difficult to beat.

Moreover, the cause of his outrage was but an orthographical error. The telegram from the Academy asked for a *Vortragstil* (a lecture style) rather than a *Vortragstitel* (a lecture title), as was intended. The telegram was mistranscribed; but the contrast between his rage at the telegram and his silence over the Holocaust suggests that he was far from a good man. But such a man could, I suppose, be a good philosopher.

It is a long way, no doubt, from Heidegger to Agatha Christie though they were very nearly contemporaries. Heidegger was born in 1889, Christie in 1890. Both died in 1976. Of course, Christie sold rather better than Heidegger, but though she was not a philosopher, yet there is philosophy to be found in her work, slipped in like a pill given to a dog in food that he likes. (It is surprising how often dogs detect the ruse, eating the food and leaving the pill. I suspect that many readers of Mrs Christie are less perceptive.)

A publisher once suggested to me that I should write a book about Christie's ideas. The idea appealed to me because it would allow me to read her oeuvre under the impression that I was working as I read one detective story after another—in order of publication, of course, to detect any evolution in her work. She was a very shrewd woman and better-read than most people today. There was less temptation in her day to distract her away from serious reading, and possibly less ideological posturing, at least among the general public.

Her style has been much criticised, as flat and formulaic, and her stories as unrealistic and frankly preposterous: but she uses concise language appropriate to what she wants to say and is frequently ironical in a pleasing and unaggressive, but sometimes pointed, way.

The unreality of her stories—their plots, their environment, their whole atmosphere—is surely part of their attraction, and why she has (allegedly) outsold all other writers of fiction in world history. Her murders are always *comfortable* rather than merely sordid as most murders are, in the sense that they are committed in the most unlikely of milieux. They upset the established order for a time, but detection restores that order, justice is done and all is right with the world once more. This is not social realism, but it is not totally divorced from the real world, either, and the fact that it is not realistic is no more a criticism than the fact that Shakespeare's historical dramas are not strictly accurate historically.

Human nature and psychology are important in Agatha Christie's books, and however lightly touched upon, the deeper questions of philosophy are present in them too.

I take as my exhibit *They Do It with Mirrors*, published in 1952.[4] I take it not because I think it is her best book—I don't think that it is—but because I happened to read it recently. Mrs Christie shows in it, however, that she is alert to the trends of her time and able gently to satirise them. She was nothing if not shrewd.

The story takes place in Stoneygates, a great Victorian pile in the country. It is run by Mr and Mrs Serrocold as a home for juvenile delinquents (as they were then called), though they are housed in separate accommodation. Mrs Serrocold has been married twice before, once to a Scandinavian magnate who left her an immense fortune, and then to an out-and-out rotter who left her for a Yugoslav dancer. Mr Serrocold, by contrast, is a solid and prosperous, but not immensely rich, accountant with philanthropic ideals and ambitions. His dream in life is to redeem juvenile delinquents and to this end he uses the foundation started by his wife's first husband—his wife always being susceptible to idealists. But Mr Serrocold turns out to be both an embezzler and a murderer, though all for his good cause. He is avid for money, but not to live luxuriously; he wants to reclaim his delinquents and set up a utopian community on an island for them. In pursuit of this

---

[4] In fact, I am currently writing a short book using this book as an illustrative template.

end, he places some of his supposedly reformed delinquents in responsible positions in companies from which they can embezzle money to be used for the purchase of the island. In other words, the end justifies the means.

1952 was perhaps the high tide of the hope that psychological treatment would be able to turn delinquents from their path of wrongdoing. I have a number of books dating from this period, suggesting that crime is actually a medico-psychological problem, and delinquents are above all in need of 'help'—by doctors, psychoanalysts, psychiatrists, social workers, and the like. This is a view that Christie gently mocks (rightly, in my view). At Stoneygates, there is a psychiatrist called Dr Maverick who is possessed of the self-proclaimed ability to understand everybody who comes under his purview. Christie is aware that the claim to be able almost instantaneously to understand everything is not only vainglorious, but a sign of understanding nothing, including its own lack of understanding. The policeman in the story, Inspector Curry, is aware of this, as Maverick is not:

> 'Oh yes, Dr Maverick will explain it all right,' said Curry grimly. 'Dr Maverick can explain everything. I'm sure of that.'

The irony here is in the implicit criticism of the claims of psychoanalysis, in essence (and more amusingly) the criticism of Karl Popper of it as what he called a *reinforced dogmatism*, a theory contrary to evidence which is not taken as a refutation but (with *ad hoc* additional hypotheses made up specially for the occasion), as a confirmation.

They Do It with Mirrors is, to a minor extent, a *roman à clef*. Dr Maverick says to Miss Marple:

> I'm sure you're going to be interested in what we're doing here in our splendid approach to this great problem. Mr Serrocold is a man of great insight—great vision. And we've got Sir John Stillwell behind us—my old chief. He was at the Home Office until he retired and his influence turned the scales in getting this started. It's a medical problem—that's what we've got to get the legal authorities to understand.

Sir John Stillwell is surely Sir William Norwood East (1872-1953), who was head of the Prison Medical Service, and who wrote such books as *The Adolescent Criminal* and *Society and the Criminal*, as well as reports for the Home Office. He was not a complete medicaliser, as is his disciple, Dr Maverick, but as Agatha Christie puts it so accurately in the latter's mouth, 'his influence turned the scale in getting this started'—this being the medicalisation of crime and the consequent therapeutic theory of punishment.

Christie satirises the facile theories and explanations of bad behaviour offered in her time, that, fundamentally, are still current. Mrs Serrocold is thoroughly in agreement with her husband when she says, in true disciple-fashion:

> Lewis says that so much of juvenile crime is due to exhibitionism, most of the boys have had such a thwarted unhappy home life, and these hold-ups and burglaries male them feel heroes.

Christie pokes fun at the idea that, with enough therapeutic endeavour, Man can be made good and society therefore perfect.

One day, if I have time and world enough, I will write an essay in which I will propose the theory that both Hercule Poirot and Miss Marple are serial killers, for what else can explain the outbreak of murder in the most unlikely places that follows them wherever they go?

In the 1970s a series of paperback books called *Modern Masters* was published by *Fontana*. They were each about 100–150 pages long, and they were biographical essays on cultural and political figures deemed important for the twentieth century (in those days, I thought that the twentieth century would last for ever). The biographical essay has always seemed to me a superior genre to that of biography in that it requires distilment, much to the advantage of the reader, though perhaps there is a graver danger of distortion or deliberate misinterpretation than with biography. There is a tendency in biography, especially nowadays, to over-inclusiveness, and there are few figures of whose maternal great-grandfather we need to know much. The biographical essay, by contrast, must concentrate on what is most significant about its subject, and avoid the strong temptation of biographers to include a fact because it had taken him so much trouble to uncover it. I know that temptation well: in one of the few pieces of original historical research that I have done, I found much information that no one before me had found. Unfortunately, it was of such a nature than no one needed to know it, either, but I included it nevertheless in my book because I did not want my effort to go to waste. This is like finishing what is on your plate when you are no longer hungry because, like Mount Everest, it is there: a waste that is worse than merely leaving your food the plate.

I took up one of my collections of *Modern Masters* the other day (surely the title of the series suggests some kind of endorsement beyond mere importance). It was that devoted to Gramsci, the Italian semi-Marxist, by James Joll, the eminent historian. I was very soon surprised, for example by the following statement:

> Problems of culture, education and philosophy were far more central to Gramsci's thought and action than they were for Tolstoy, while he was far more directly involved in political practice and organization than Lukacs was.

This is an extraordinary thing to have written. I am not an historian, but even I know that Gyorgy Lukacs was a minister in the brief Hungarian revolutionary regime of 1919, when a considerable part of his practice consisted of signing death warrants (which were carried out). Moreover, he was profoundly implicated and involved in practical politics for the rest of his life, far longer and deeper than Gramsci ever was— no doubt because Gramsci was in prison for the last eleven years of his life, with practically no opportunity to affect practical politics. One cannot help sympathising with Gramsci on a human level: born into poverty, at least by any of today's standards, he suffered from Pott's disease—tuberculosis—of the spine, which made him a hunchback and must have caused him immense physical suffering, a fact not emphasised in Joll's book. Gramsci died young, at 45, not long before he was to be provisionally released. Along with Alexander Pope, who suffered the same disease, he might have written the line, which is true rather than self-pitying, 'This long disease, my life.'

Gramsci is considered a Marxist writer and theoretician, but I think that his most important theory, or idea, namely that of the importance of intellectuals' and cultural elites' ability to bring about revolutionary social and economic change, was not only not Marxist, but was anti-Marxist. The proposition could have occurred to anyone without Marxist verbiage about the dialectic, or the *Dialectic*, upon which he lavished so much wasted mental effort. The famous, or infamous, long march through the institutions, for which he is now best-known for having propounded, required no Marxist verbiage to explain or even predict it. And when one considers how quickly ideas that shortly before would have seemed bizarre or outrageous, are now adopted as orthodoxies by institutions, it would perhaps be better to speak of the short flood though the institutions.

Joll's book was published in 1977 (in nominal terms, it too cost much less than a postage stamp today). I don't think that anyone would now write: 'his attempts… to find a new form of revolutionary organization which could continue effective leadership with real participation by the rank and file, have all been cited to show how the doctrines of Marx and Lenin might be used in ways different from those followed by Stalin.' Marx was, at least in theory, bloodthirsty, though he never had the opportunity to put his bloodthirstiness into practice, and, to give him the benefit of the doubt, he might well have shrunk in horror from it had he actually seen or experienced it first-hand; but the same cannot be said of Lenin, with his neurosyphilis perhaps as an excuse or explanation. If Lenin had objected to Stalin's murderousness, it would have been on the grounds that the wrong people were being murdered, not on any bourgeois-sentimental grounds that to kill large numbers of people is wrong in itself. Every reference to Lenin in the book suggests that he was qualitatively different from Stalin in point of brutality and attitude to the sanctity of individual human life, but this was clearly not so. In 1977, however (three years after the publication of *The Gulag Archipelago* in Britain), this was not understood, at least not by some academics. 'Faced with what was done by Stalin and his successors in the name of Marx and Lenin...', writes Joll elsewhere in the book, again suggesting a categorical ethical difference between them. This, it seems to me (though I am by no means a specialist in the subject), was a rather fundamental misunderstanding of the Russian Revolution and its aftermath. Dostoyevsky and Conrad wrote before both the revolution and its aftermath with more understanding than Joll, who had the supposed advantage of hindsight.

It is odd how a decent man, brilliantly intelligent as was Joll, could get things so wrong. Twelve years before the fall of the Berlin Wall and the subsequent—and consequent—decline of the Italian Communist Party (in 1991, I bought a book in Italy by a psychotherapist about how Italian communists could overcome their grief at the loss of their ideals and love objects), Joll wrote: 'The Italian Communists can perhaps claim that they are well on their way to establishing their hegemony with the collapse of the old [capitalist] system.' Whatever may have happened since, it has not been the hegemony of the Italian Communist Party in Italy.

Joll seems sometimes not even to appreciate the import of the words that he quotes. Gramsci was an admirer of Machiavelli and wanted to write a modern, up-to-date *Prince*. The Prince would not be an individual but a political party:

> The modern Prince, as it develops, revolutionizes the whole system of intellectual and moral relations, in that its development means precisely that any given act is seen as useful or harmful, as virtuous or wicked, only in so far as it has its point of reference the modern Prince itself, and helps to strengthen or to oppose it. In man's consciences, the Prince takes the place of the divinity or the categorical imperative...

This is as compatible with Nazism as with communism, and only a man with an understanding enfeebled by excessive theorising about such things as the dialectic could fail to realise the modern Prince was atrocious.

If someone wanted to learn how to write good English prose, he could do worse than to read Eric Ambler. In literary matters, Ambler was self-trained, the best training anyone could have, and his prose is elegant and highly literate. He wrote mainly political thrillers, which perhaps explains why no one would study him for purely literary enlightenment. He started out in engineering, and though he never practised as an engineer, it might have given him a taste for exactitude.

Ambler (1909-1998) was an ironist. His autobiography, written when he was 76 and therefore likely to have had death on his mind, has the wonderfully ambiguous title, *Here Lies Eric Ambler*, referring to his future burial and to the fact that no autobiography is the truth, the whole truth, and nothing but the truth, however much the author might desire it to be.

His novel, *Judgement on Deltchev*, was inspired by the show trials in the newly-constituted communist regimes of Eastern Europe (Ambler had previously been somewhat sympathetic to the Soviet regime). Published in 1951, it begins:

> Where treason to the state is defined simply as opposition to the government in power, the political leader convicted of it will not necessarily lose credit with the people. Indeed, if he is respected or loved by them, his death at the hands of a tyrannical government may serve to give his life a dignity it did not before possess.

Probably Ambler's most famous book, though, is *The Mask of Demetrios*, published in America under the inferior title, *A Coffin for Demetrios*. Not only does the latter title give the denouement away, but it is less euphonious. The question is why editors and publishers so often find it necessary to make changes for the worse? No one could object to changes for the better, but it often seems a matter of chance whether they are for the better or worse. Why, then? I suppose editors and publishers feel about books the way dogs feel about trees: they want to make their mark on them. It is the nearest they come to creativity and working as they do in a creative field—or a supposedly creative field—they feel some kind of creation-envy. A good editor is above the price of rubies, but a bad one is below the price of rotting fish.

The Mask of Demetrios begins, as does *Judgement on Deltchev*, with some ironical reflections on human affairs. Chance, says Ambler, plays an underestimated part in such affairs; but some people insist that all is providential. 'For the sceptic, there remains only one consolation: if there should be such a thing as a super-human Law, it is administered with subhuman inefficiency.' And he says of the hero or protagonist of his book (not quite the same thing), that 'The choice of Latimer as its instrument could have been made only by an idiot.'

Latimer is a former university lecturer in economics who was of the great army of university professors 'who write detective novels in their spare time,' but he 'soon emerged as one of the shamefaced few who could make money at the sport.' He gave up economics for murder, no doubt equally fictitious at first; but then, intrigued by the story of the corpse fished out of the Bosphorus which he happened to be visiting at the time, he decides to turn real, if still amateur, detective. The Demetrios of the title is a kind of multidisciplinary criminal, a Greek from Ottoman Turkey, who ranges from what used to be called the white slave trade to political assassination and heroin smuggling.

The novel was published in 1939, when war in Europe was again certain. There are a few things in the book that surprised me. Demetrios killed a Jewish money-lender in Smyrna in 1922, the year in which the militarily-defeated Greeks agreed to an exchange of populations with the Turks, 1,200,000 against 400,000. This was, of course, a year of massacre also, especially in Smyrna (from which my wife's paternal family, apparently Armenian rather than Greek, descends). And yet, in the midst of all this chaos and death, the murder committed by Demetrios was investigated by the Turkish police, who co-operated with the Greek police in this matter. Is this plausible, was it possible? It appears *prima facie* unlikely, but in the other historical details of the book—for example, the assassination of the Bulgarian Prime Minister, Stambulisky, in 1923, and the reasons for it, Amber is extremely accurate. It would be surprising then if he had not based the story of a murdered Jewish money-lender on a real case.

Not long ago, I read a short book by a French academic, Vincent Duclert, *Arménie: Un genocide sans fin et le monde qui s'éteint* (Armenia: A Genocide without End and the World Extinguished), about the recent short wat between Azerbaijan and Armenia, fought over the Armenian enclave of Nagorno-Karabakh. The author suggests that it was but an episode in the nearly century-old attempt of Turkey to eliminate Armenia and the Armenians altogether, once and for all. In the course of his book, he suggests that the massacre of Armenians that continued after its apogee in 1915-16 had been expunged from western memory, presumably in an attempt to improve relations with a resurgent Turkey. But this means that Professor Duclert could not have been a close reader of Ambler, for in 1939 Ambler wrote what happened, or was done, to the Armenians in 1922:

Dragged from their houses and hiding places, men,

women and children were butchered in the streets, which soon became littered with mutilated bodies. The wooden walls of the churches, packed with refugees, were drenched with benzene and fired. The occupants who were not burned alive were bayoneted as they tried to escape.

One cannot accuse Ambler of frivolity, even as he tries to entertain.

But he can be funny. At the beginning of the novel, Latimer encounters Colonel Hakim, the chief of the Turkish secret police in 1939:

> He [Hakim] could not be less than fifty, Latimer thought, and studied the waist below the beautifully cut officer's uniform in the hope of detecting the corsets.

There are many small delights in reading Ambler, as well as the pleasures of the plot. Latimer goes with Colonel Hakim to the post-mortem of the body fished out of the Bosphorus:

> The mortuary was a small, corrugated-iron building in the precinct of the police station near the mosque of Nouri Osmanieh... The afternoon heat had set the air above the concrete yard quivering and Latimer began to wish that he had not come. It was not the weather for visiting corrugated-iron mortuaries.

Later, inside the mortuary, Latimer makes the rather obvious observation that it was very hot. 'The Colonel shrugged and nodded towards the trestles [on which were placed the bodies]. "They don't complain."'

This put me in mind of the time I was in Nottingham. I found the best place in the city to be the municipal cemetery. One day walking in it, I noticed a young gardener working with great care and attention, the kind that only people who love their work can pay.

'You like your work,' I said to him.

'The residents are well-behaved,' he said.

This was more than could be said for all the residents of Nottingham.

Eric Ambler was born in London in 1909, two months after my father was born there. In the month of my father's birth, April, there took place in Adana and its surrounds, in what was then called Cilicia, a massacre of between 20,000 and 30,000 Armenians. In 1911, the Armenian writer, Zabel Essayan (or Yessayan) wrote a book about it in Armenian, translated a century later into French, titled *Dans les ruines: Le massacre d'Adana avril 1909* (In the Ruins: the Adana Massacre, April 1909). It is a book to make you tremble for humanity.

Essayan (1878-1943) was an educated member of the Francophile Armenian middle class. She studied in Paris and sometimes wrote in French: she was at least trilingual, in Armenian, Turkish and French. She must have been able to read fluently in three very different scripts: the Armenian, Ottoman Turkish and Latin. This was in itself an accomplishment.

The background to the massacre was this: in 1908, the Committee of Union and Progress (CUP), or Young Turks, overthrew the government of the Sultan, Abdulhamid. They promised—once again—equality to all the subjects of the Ottoman Empire without regard to their ethnicity or religion. This aroused great enthusiasm in the intelligentsia, particularly the Armenians. In April, 1909, however, there was a military uprising to restore Abdulhamid's power and the Charia. It was quickly and ferociously put down by the CUP, but the uprising fanned the hopes of the Turks of Cilicia, who were still attached to the old regime. A vote would not have resulted in the victory of liberalism.

Armenians had among them not only peasants but relatively well-to-do merchants and landowners. Resentment against supposed inferiors who were now, de facto, superiors was very great, but no mere explanation can do justice to what happened. There will always be a gap between what is to be explained and the explanation.

Essayan went, at the request of the Armenian Orthodox Church, to investigate the condition of the thousands of Armenian children orphaned by the massacre, three months after it. Her book is an account of what she saw and heard. It almost passes belief—except that we know it is true, or possible, because it has happened (with variations) several times since.

When it comes to monstrosity, there is no linear scale to measure it. In a sense, it would be 'better' if 20,000 had been massacred rather than 30,000, but one would hardly claim that there was a huge moral difference between the two.

Hence it is not easy to extract the most startling,

heartbreaking passage of this book. Time and again the survivors say that they would rather have been blind and deaf than to have seen and heard what they witnessed.

The massacres were spontaneous, like pogroms, but the authorities either cooperated with them or did little to restrain them. After they were over and the Armenian quarters of the town and villages had been totally destroyed, the authorities arrested surviving Armenians and accused them of having resisted by resort to arms, as if there had been any other way to resist. They publicly hanged some of them without enquiring as to whether they had actually been 'guilty' of armed resistance. As he mounted the collective gibbet, one young man sang a song and his last words were that he was guilty because he had betrayed the hope placed in him precisely because he had failed to take up arms.

The French edition of the book contains photographs, including of a contemporary postcard showing a gibbet with a soldier standing in front of it, four of the hanged men dangling from the crossbeam. The postcard bears the legend ADANA, as it might have done if it were from a holiday destination, with the words Kassap, Missuh and Hatdsou, the names of three of the hanged, also. What is most astonishing, however, is that the postcard has been stamped (on the picture side) and franked ADANA 10-6-1913, and presumably sent to the addressee—from Ottoman Turkey itself.

What, if anything, can we conclude from this? That in 1913, Ottoman Turkey believed in freedom of expression and opinion? Or that its authorities saw nothing wrong in what had been done, indeed were proud of it? Or that they were so sure of themselves that they cared not at all for the opinion of the world? Or that the CUP wanted to show what was the alternative to themselves?

Those to whom Essayan spoke were wiser than she. They had seen the massacres of 1895 and 1909 and did not believe that any mere political change would now alter the Turkish hatred of them or prevent them from being massacred again. One of them told her to flee, to flee for her life, which she had to do in 1915, barely escaping. She then spent years in Belgium and France, before going to Soviet Armenia to live, believing in the Soviet promise of freedom. In 1937, she was arrest and accused of being a nationalist. She was imprisoned in Yerevan and Baku, and then disappeared in 1943, never to be heard of again. Witness to massacre, then to genocide, then to mass purges in the land of the Soviets! La Rochefoucauld said that we can stare neither at the sun nor death for very long: nor can we bear to contemplate the fate of Zabel Essayan.

One passage in the book has a special meaning for me. Essayan visits the church in a town called Osmaniye:

> We arrived at last at the church: four walls having been licked by the flames and the ground covered with white ashes. The unfortunates who had taken refuge here had all died, burnt alive... Little bits of charred bone... what extinguished life, what snuffed out enthusiasm did they represent? On the wall, we found an inscription written in blood [on a part not blackened by the flames]. The inscription began 'The massacre started on 3 April...' Under the first line was written 'Light! Light! Light!...' His third and last line, 'God no longer exists!'

I hope I shall be forgiven if I quote from my own book, published in 1992, about my visit to Monrovia during the Liberian Civil War. I visited St Peter's Lutheran Church.

Outside St Peter's a notice still stands:

COME AND LET US GLORIFY GOD TOGETHER … In a small garden in front of the church there are two slight mounds, long and narrow. They are the mass graves of about half of about the six hundred people who took refuge in St Peter's and were massacred there in July, 1990. I entered the church, which was open. There were no pews or chairs, just empty floor space. On the walls, the numbers of the hymns were still posted: 532 and 191. The concrete wall was covered with a blackish substance, dry and in some places powdery. I looked a little closer: it had a reddish or maroon hue. It was blood. Towards the walls, one could make out silhouettes in the blood, silhouettes of bodies in contact with the ground where the blood had consequently been unable to run. I was seeing it nine or ten months after the killing, and no one had yet cleaned the floor.

Zebel Essayan visited another church where 'we still see the bloody handprints on the walls.' This was eighty-one years before the massacre at St Peter's church.

Never again say never again!

It is probable that ninety-nine of a hundred people in the west who have any knowledge of Botswana (the hundred themselves being a small minority) derive it from Alexander McCall Smith's series of books about Mma Ramotswe of the No. 1 Ladies' Detective Agency. These delightful books achieved the difficult feat of making someone good seem interesting. For every interesting hero in literature, there are a hundred interesting villains. Why this should be is itself an interesting question.

I think I may fairly claim to have been the first critic in a national publication to praise the invention of Mma Ramotswe. I knew the author socially a very little, but my praise was genuine and in no sense a favour to him. If I had not thought his book as charming as it was, I should have declined to say anything about it. But whenever I met him thereafter, I said to him, as a kind of standing joke, that if I had known that he was going to be so successful (according to Wikipedia, he has sold 40,000,000 books worldwide since), I should never have given him so favourable a review.

There is another writer about Botswana who has achieved some fame, though not quite as much as McCall Smith. He is Norman Rush, who is now aged ninety. From 1978 and 1983 he was director of the American Peace Corps in Botswana, and it was this experience that served him as a well, or mine, for his subsequent writing. Obviously, his time in Botswana was for him what would now be called a life-changing experience.

His first book, a collection of short stories, was published in 1986. They concern expatriate life in Botswana and are considerably less cheerful than McCall Smith's stories. Perhaps the twelve years that separated the publication of

Whites from *The No. 1 Ladies' Detective Agency* account in part for this difference. By the date of the latter, 1998, Botswana had developed into prosperity, and was one of the few African states that had not known dictatorship. There was reason for it to be optimistic.

Norman Rush, who had spent many years as an antiquarian bookseller, emerged as a fully-fledged writer, without much in the way of apprentice-work. He is indeed an excellent stylist, and his stories about the goldfish-bowl existence of expatriates in a country unknown to most readers are like meditations on human nature. He is far from the first author to see expatriate life as a kind of isolating laboratory of human nature—one thinks of Joseph Conrad, Stefan Zweig and Somerset Maugham, among others—but I think he belongs in their pantheon.

One unusual achievement in the book, however, is the story *Thieving*, in which a young African recounts his philosophy of theft, which is by no means simply an expression of greed. He (the author) tells the story in the words of an African who is not fully fluent in English, and it seems to me that he has achieved the difficult task (as difficult as making a good person interesting) of pitching it exactly right, authentic without condescension, mockery or excessive pity. In this respect, he equals Amos Tutuola (*The Palm-Wine Drinkard*) or Ken Saro-Wiwa (*Sozaboy: A Novel in Rotten English*). Perhaps the cultural Jacobins of the west would now accuse Rush of 'cultural appropriation', of having no right to write through the eyes of an African: but this would be an absurd criticism which, if taken to its logical conclusion, would make all fictional narratives, except those strictly in the first person, impossible.

Moreover, there would be no point in such fiction because it could convey nothing of anyone else's experience to the reader. Everyone would be enclosed, imprisoned, in mental solitary confinement. In fact, the effort would be worse than pointless, it would be harmful insofar as it fooled readers into the supposition that he or she *could* understand the viewpoint of another person from within.

But let me carp for a moment (how I love carping!). In the first story in the book, there is an error that I am surprised that the editors of the *New Yorker*, in which it first appeared, let pass. The error in question is the confusion of *baroque* and *feudal*. The story is titled *Bruns* and begins:

> Poor Bruns. They hated him so much it was baroque. But then so is Ketang baroque, everything about it. Probably the Boers were going to hate Bruns no matter what. Boers ran Ketang, they've been there for generations.

A little further, Rush writes:

> The Boers got used to doing what they wanted, black government or not. They still pay their farm labor in sugar and salt and permission to crawl underneath their cows and suck fresh milk. It is baroque.

He meant feudal, not baroque: but then I remind myself that pedantry is often how one keeps thoughts of one's own mediocrity at bay.

The longest story in the book, *Official Americans*, is a wonderfully subtle and accurate dissection of the mentality

and society of a small group of expatriates in a far-flung place
(far-flung for the expatriates, nowhere is far-flung to natives of
the place). In this story, we witness—so persuasive is the
narrative—the breakdown of a 56-year-old man, Frank, a
career foreign-aidist, if I may so put it, who is married for the
second time, now to a much younger woman with a New Age
attitude to life, especially in medical matters. Frank's job is to
promote small businesses and entrepreneurship. He works for
the American embassy, where the ambassador is almost a god-
like figure who must be obeyed, appeased and persuaded that
he, Frank, is doing a good job. Frank's divorce from his first
wife was so costly that he could not afford to return to America
even if he wanted to so because he needs all the advantages
and perquisites, including housing, that attach to a foreign
posting.

He is allocated a Botswanan government house next door
to the Minister of Labour's house. The minister has several
dogs who keep Frank awake at night with their barking (they
sleep all day). Frank attributes his woes to his insomnia caused
by the dogs, but the minister flatly refuses to do anything about
them. Frank is persuaded by the wife of another employee of
the embassy, who has an interest in Botswanan folk medicine
and magic, to consult a local witch doctor. Frank goes through
with it, in the hope that the *muti* (the word for such medicine
that I still remember from my days in Rhodesia nearly fifty
years ago) will drive away or quieten the dogs, enabling him
to sleep and be happy. His situation is so desperate that he is
willing to try what he would once have scoffed at.

It doesn't turn out well. The witch doctor is a charlatan and
not local at all. His ceremonies are bogus and rely for their

performance on Frank's credulity. Among other things, the supposed witch doctor scarifies Frank's back and rubs something into the wounds. Frank develops septicaemia. He takes or is given some neomycin that has been left lying about the house and (an accurate detail) it causes deafness in one of his ears.

No mere synopsis can capture the subtlety of Rush's writing and the acuteness of his observation. Perhaps I am so impressed because I have lived something approximate to the way of life that he describes, and from which he drew his inspiration, but I hope not. A writer as good as he can convey not only a country's atmosphere but a whole way of life in a paragraph.

When I was young, I thought that I would like to be a bohemian, but by the time I was old enough to become one, it was no longer possible. Property prices had risen so much, and of course rents with them, that it was no longer possible to rent a dingy room in the centre of a metropolis and live on next to nothing, meeting in cheap cafés and accommodating pubs where credit was offered. Practically everyone now has more possessions than he can conveniently carry with him when he is evicted from lodgings—besides which, eviction from where one is living is now almost impossible, certainly not quick, which means that lodgings are harder, or even impossible, to find. Easy come, easy go: hard to go, hard to come. To rent a room in Paris, you have not only to put down a hefty deposit and prove that you have a regular and sufficient income to pay the exorbitant rent, but you need references and a guarantor, also sufficiently well-off, to pay your rent should you abscond or otherwise fail as a tenant. This is not conducive to *la vie de bohème*, to say the least.

Jean Rhys's novel, *After Leaving Mr Mackenzie*, published in 1930, is redolent of a world in which bohemianism was still possible. The dinginess and discomfort, the financial precariousness, of this way of life, was the *quid pro quo* for the freedom it offered. If there is luxury in it, then it is not of material goods but of time. There was nothing that absolutely had to be done, at a particular time. Even in the cheapest hotel, which would appal us nowadays, so used have we become to private bathrooms, there was service of a kind, in which breakfast was served by a blowsy and resentful maid, in residents' bedrooms. There was discomfort and a lack of accoutrements that we regard as indispensable, but there was also a freedom almost unknown to anyone now. The general increase in the standard of living has enslaved us, at least those of us who might once have been bohemians. Now we feel oppressed by our belongings, accumulated over the years, that we have not the courage to dispense with.

The protagonist of Jean Rhys's book, Julia Martin, lives the bohemian life without its intellectual or artistic pretensions. She has escaped from London to the far more glamorous Paris, but her life is one of constant anxiety and fear of destitution. She lives hand-to-mouth and has absolutely no reserves. We see her first in an area of Paris that I know well, the Sixth arrondissement, because I used to stay there on my regular visits to the city, cheaply as I thought, but very expensively by comparison with Julia's budget.

In essence, Julia lives off men, though, now in her mid-thirties, this will become more and more difficult. The men with whom she has associated were all rotters in one way or another; and the Mr Mackenzie of the title discards her, agreeing to pay her 300 francs a month, but then sending her a cheque for 1500 francs in full and final payment, as it were. Her search is now on for funds from elsewhere. Her decline in attractiveness is brilliantly captured in a scene in which a young man approaches her, assuming her to be a woman of easy virtue but, taking one look at her face, decides against making a proposition. Incidentally, morals were looser in the Sixth arrondissement of 1930 than they are now, one more effect of general prosperity.

Julia has a sister, Norah, who has stayed in London (in Acton, actually, a suburb hovering between poverty and respectability), and looks after their incapacitated, demented mother. Norah has a lodger and companion whom one would nowadays not hesitate to assume was a lesbian. Julia and Norah detest one another, Julia ascribing her sister's hostility to jealousy. True, Norah is financially somewhat more secure than Julia, but her life is entirely circumscribed by the care she is obliged to give to their mute mother. She is much less free than Julia and therefore has cause to envy her even as she disapproves of her way of life, which she assumes to be dissolute and decadent.

I suppose feminists would say that the two sisters represent the twin poles of female experience in 1930: domestic drudgery on the one hand, or *de facto* prostitution on the other. I am unsure how far this is an accurate summary, sociologically, of the position and experience of women in

1930: it seems rather schematic to me, though not without a certain validity if one remembers that it is a caricature without statistical validity. And perhaps it ought to be remembered that the position of men in 1930 wasn't all that jolly, either.

There is no sentimentality in the book, however, because Julia is not a very sympathetic character. She is hard as nails and the possibility of being other than a parasite does not occur to her. She can be charming, but she cannot keep it up. She is by nature completely uncompromising, which makes any lasting liaison impossible. At no point does she feel any affection or sympathy for others. Moreover, she is uninterested in anything other than the day-to-day flux of her own existence, albeit that she can spend much of the day in her cheap hotel bedroom reading (but what, one wonders?). She is inclined to drink too much, in which she resembles her creator.

The writing is taut, as is the construction of the book. Its outlook is completely bleak, without either hope or nostalgia for a better life. One feels that this is just the world as it is and that it cannot be otherwise.

Oddly enough, such a book does not depress, at least depress me. I find optimism much more depressing than pessimism, perhaps because the latter leads to acceptance of the imperfections around one. In addition, such a book confronts me, who am such a lamenter of the state of the world, with evidence of the real progress that has taken place. Here is a description of the maid who brings Julia her breakfast in her cheap hotel:

She was a big, fair girl, sullen and rather malicious

because she worked without stopping from six in the morning until eleven or twelve at night, and because she knew that, being plain, she would probably have to work like that until she died.

I don't think that anyone could write such a description nowadays and be expected to be believed. Living on social security, bad as it is, is surely better than this. The world moves on, but human nature remains the same.

There is little more delightful reading, though, than that about the foolishness of people in the past. It is not only amusing in itself but serves to reassure us that we could never be so foolish ourselves, so credulous or gullible. No: we, at last, are rational creatures, unsusceptible to charlatanry.

Among the most delightful books about credulity known to me are two published by the British Medical Association in 1909 (the year of my father's birth) and 1913. They are titled *Secret Remedies: What They Cost and What They Contain*, and *More Secret Remedies*. My copy of the first of these titles says that it is of the hundred and fifth thousandth sold: if true, a real best-seller of the time.

The book contains the name, description, chemical analysis and advertising claims made on behalf of the secret remedies. Dull would he be of soul who could not respond to the poetry of the names of the remedies, of which I give the briefest of selection:

Hargreave's Reducing Wafers, Zox, Gower's Green Pills, Professor O. Phelps Brown's Vervain Restorative, Assimilant, Dr Van Vech's Complete Absorptive Pile Treatment, Fitch's Kidney and Liver Cooler, Gloria Treatment for Rheumatism, Captain Fielder's Crimson Cross No. 1 Ointment, Nurse Mann's Remedy, Towle's Pennyroyal and Steel Pills, Mrs Stafford-Brookes' Pelloids, Juvenia.

The full list is very long.

The selling price of these remedies is compared with the cost of their contents, no allowance being made for overheads or costs of promotion. The most egregious examples sell at a thousand times the cost of the ingredients; but the introduction to the first volume pays a kind of tribute to the placebo effect, that eternal ally of both the doctor and the quack:

It must not be assumed that the concoctors of these mixtures and powders and ointments show any particular skill in the compounding of drugs. On the contrary, they appear curiously indifferent to taste and appearance, and perhaps count on the belief, common among the poorer classes at least, that the nastier a drug the more effective it is. There is, at any rate, the excuse for this belief that the effect to subdue the repugnance to the draught produces a glow of virtue which might perhaps have a certain stimulating effect on the mind; the patient not only having spent his money but suffered some discomfort, is anxious to justify his faith by assuming himself to be the better for the double sacrifice.

Medicine may have made advances, but not the prose of doctors, or at least that of the British Medical Association. The introduction to the book begins:

> One of the reasons for the popularity of secret remedies is their secrecy. It is a can in which the old saying Omne ignotum pro magnifica [Everything unknown is held to be magnificent, a saying from Tacitus] applies. To begin with, there is for the average man or woman a certain fascination in secrecy. The quack takes advantage of this common foible of human nature to impress his customers. But secrecy has other uses in his trade; it enables him to make use of cheaper new or old fashioned drugs, and to proclaim that his product possesses virtues beyond the ken of the mere doctor; his herbs have been culled from in some remote prairie in America or among the mountains of Central Africa, the secret of their virtues having been confided in him by some venerable chief; or again he will have us believe that his drug has been discovered by chemical research of alchemical profundity, and is produced by processes so costly and elaborate that it can be sold only at a very high price.

Plus ça change. We may have advanced in many directions, but not in all.

I had assumed that obesity had only recently been considered a disease, but I was mistaken. In the literature enclosed with *Antipon*, a treatment for obesity, we find the following: 'Antipon absolutely and definitely replaces all the weakening and frequently dangerous processes, systems and medicines which hitherto have done duty as remedies for the disease of obesity.'

Nelson Lloyd, in the literature accompanying the *Nelson Lloyd Safe Reducing Treatment*, goes in for confessional mode: 'I myself am a member of a family many of whom died prematurely after much mental and physical suffering, arising from corpulence. While studying medicine for my degree, I saw signs of the family complaint in myself. I naturally sought to avert what I for some time feared as being my hereditary fate… I gave up expecting a cure from other people. I experimented with my own thought-out remedies, and, happily, at last my perseverance—or rather my desperation—succeeded…'

This rather reminded me of the story of M. Boursin, a cheesemaker in Normandy, who spent many years, according to the information on the packaging, developing the formula for the cheese that has conquered the world—though it is far from a cure for obesity.

These books make wonderful reading. Chapter XIX of the first is titled *Cures for Inebriety*. Among them are *Dipsocure*, *Antidipso* and *Teetolia*. In Dipsocure's accompanying pamphlet, we read, 'Eminent medical men have over and over again declared that if a cure for drunkenness could be discovered both TASTELESS and ODOURLESS and placed in the hands of a devoted woman to be administered SECRETLY, the greatest difficulty in effecting cures would have been overcome.'

The powder of Dipsocure contained acetanilide, potassium

bromide (a sedative) and lactulose. As for the Teetolia Treatment, the discovery of its 'method and treatment for the permanent eradication of the craving for drink and drugs marks an era in medical science'. Furthermore, 'You can, while undergoing the treatment, pursue your ordinary methods of living. You continue to take your daily modicum of alcohol; but somehow about the third or fourth day of treatment, without having made any physical or mental effort, you feel that you no longer want a drink; it holds out no attraction to you; its magnetic influence is gone…!'

Perhaps one of the reasons for Teetolia's success was that it contained 29.3 per cent alcohol, which might at least guarantee future sales.

But the BMA of 1909 and 1913 saw the beams but not the motes. The drugs in the official pharmacopoeia of the time were mostly useless—from today's standpoint—and probably often harmful. Furthermore, the evidence in favour of the official medicines was often testimonial in nature, albeit the testimonial of doctors rather than of patients.

In the first week of 2024, I bought in a Parisian bookshop two books that had been published in that week. I was exultant in a quiet but foolish way. I knew it to be absurd, for nothing is more fleeting than the newness of new publications, or for that matter the newness of new years. I have always found the firework celebration of the new year a little odd: for usually the new year will soon prove that there was nothing to celebrate, except perhaps the feat of having survived thus far.

One of the two books I bought was *Papa, qu'est ce qu'on a fait au Rwanda?* (Daddy, What Did We Do in Rwanda?), by Laurent Larcher. It is written as a series of letters to the author's daughter: it is time, he says, as she enters adulthood that she should know about this important subject. And indeed, compared to genocide all other subjects are inclined to appear trivial, almost frivolous. But if we never turned our minds to less important subjects, the consequences would be very serious.

It so happens that the evening before I bought and read this short book, I had seen a German film, *Der Wannseekonferenz*, The Wannseekonferenz, the majority of which was a brilliant and literal reconstruction of the meeting, under the chairmanship of Reinhard Heydrich, which took the decision to kill all the Jews in Europe. One sees the highly educated civil servants, lawyers and academics considering the matter as if it were a municipal matter such as better street-lighting, raising only practical, not moral, objections—with the exception of one participant who appeared to have scruples, but was nonetheless careful to present his objections as pragmatic rather than moral. The whole is so brilliantly played that one feels at the end that one was actually present at the conference (it was filmed in the mansion where it actually took place). The complete calm with which outwardly civilised people could contemplate the killing of 11 million people, as they thought or hoped to do, and the 'rationality' with which they did so, was chilling in the extreme—more chilling, perhaps, than any direct representation of the results of their deliberation would have been.

It is the contention of the book about Rwanda, very well

written, that the French government under the leadership of François Mitterrand, was similarly cold-blooded about the events in Rwanda between 1990 and 1994. According to the author, it believed that the *Front Patriotique Rwandais* (the Rwandan Patriotic Front), that invaded Rwanda from Uganda, made up of Tutsis who had long taken refuge in that country, was a catspaw for the Anglos-Saxons to penetrate Francophone Africa and destroy France's almost unopposed influence in that very large area.[5] The French government therefore was prepared to support the Francophone and Francophile regime of Juvénal Habyarimana to the bitter end, despite the knowledge that it was genocidal in nature.

Again, according to the author, Mitterrand and his government were aware from the first that there was a risk of genocide in Rwanda if the FPR continued to make inroads into the country. There had been periodical massacres of Tutsis before, from the very time of independence from Belgium. But if the French knew the risk, surely the FPR knew it also: they decided nonetheless that the light was worth the candle and went ahead.

The question naturally arises as to how far those who knew this might happen if they proceeded in a certain way were to some degree responsible for what happened when they did so proceed. This is a very difficult question. If a man comes up to me in the street and says, 'I will stab you if you don't hand over your money,' and I believe him but nevertheless don't

---

[5] Since opposed by the Russian mercenary army, the so-called Wagner Group.

hand over my money, am I co-responsible when he stabs me? Surely not. It is no defence if someone steals from a car that the owner had left something in the car and the window open. Yet at the same time you would not recommend that someone left his belongings in a car with the window open when it was known that there were thieves about, and you would feel somewhat less sympathy for him if that is what he did and his belongings were stolen.

The author does not mention either that the FPR did not invade Rwanda only that there could be an equitable division of government posts, land or anything else between the two main ethnic groups, but that they, the FPR, might constitute a new government. He does not mention either that the Hutu might have reason to fear this, because only twenty years or so earlier, in the mirror-image country of Burundi, there had been a massacre by a Tutsi government of every Hutu who had attended secondary school. I doubt that this had any part in the French government's calculations, for Mitterrand was a Machiavellian's Machiavellian (I think he probably preferred intrigue for its own sake to straightforwardness, as there are some swindlers who would prefer to make a small amount of money dishonestly than a large one honestly); but such considerations as I have here, with some trepidation, put forward might serve to complicate the picture in the mind of the author's daughter, and incline her less to a burden of guilt, a guilt for something for what she was not in the least responsible.

Most people have enough reasons to feel guilty for their own personal acts or omissions without an extra burden placed on them for the past actions of their country, that they would not have been able to avert even had they been alive at the time.

Nor does the book deal with the question of how far Paul Kagame and his FPR had been responsible for the war in the eastern Congo, which has killed, or lead to the deaths, of millions of people. I recently read a book by the Cameroonian political scientist, Charles Onana, which claimed that Kagame, imbued with the idea of Tutsi superiority and therefore right to rule, planned the war in the eastern Congo from the first, in order to lay his, or Rwanda's hands on its vital mineral resources.[6]

Do I have an opinion on this matter? Should I, can I, do I *need* to have an opinion on this matter?

The second of the books published early in 2024 which I was so proud to have bought so near to their date of publication was a kind of intelligent pot-boiler titled *À la table des tyrans*, At the Dinner Table of Tyrants, by Christian Roudaut. It consists of six longish essays on six tyrants' taste in food: Mao, Hitler, Stalin, the Emperor Bokassa and Saddam Hussein.

It is obvious that we cannot get enough of tyrants—on paper. Who cares what Harold Wilson or Margaret Thatcher, etc. ate, or how they behaved at dinner parties? The menus of Jimmy Carter would be of about as much interest as the train timetables from London to Hemel Hempstead in 1973. But

---

[6] Onana has since been charged with the offence of apology for genocide. Whether this should be considered an offence is a thorny question.

somehow we want to know every last detail of these six characters' lives (and many others of similar ilk that we could think of), though we don't care about such details of the lives of anyone else.

I recall quite vividly when Jean-Bedel Bokassa declared that he was going to crown himself Emperor. I was working in a small lunatic asylum in the East End of London at the time, and here was a completely different kind of lunacy, probably unique in modern history.[7] I seem to remember—though it is possible that it is a false memory—that, among other extravagances, Bokassa ordered £50,000 worth (or was it dollars or francs?) of rose petals to be flown in from Paris to be strewn in his path in Bangui, the capital, on the great day. I also seem to remember from my stamp-collecting days that attar of roses came mainly from Bulgaria. Whether rose petals can ever worth £50,000 depends, I suppose, on whether you use market- or use-value as the measure.

Anyhow, I thought of taking two weeks' holiday to attend that great and unrepeatable event but, ever of lazy disposition, I did not get around to arranging it. How I now wish that I had! There have been few events as bizarre since, though in a country as poor as the Central African Republic (soon to be Empire), such expenditure was far from having been *only* bizarre. The Emperor was betrayed in the end by—what to call them exactly?—his sponsors in France. Exiled in a chateau there but with no means to run it, he suffered the same fate as Jean-Claude Duvalier, Baby Doc. It is difficult,

[7] The coronation in 1928 of King Zog as king of Albania was comparatively sane.

however, to sympathise too greatly with a man who fathered fifty-seven children and whose only way to feed them was to loot a country. But, as Sor Juana Inés de la Cruz asked in the seventeenth century, who is more to blame, he who pays for sin, or he who sins for pay? So long as he was useful, Bokassa found powerful friends abroad.

Of course, there is the question of Bokassa's alleged cannibalism. Of this, the author of *À la table des tyrans* remains sceptical. He writes:

> On 11 October 1979, Libération [the then far-leftist French newspaper] had the headline, Bokassa, an African Bluebeard, founding it on the sulphurous revelation of Jacques Duchemin. This Frenchman, briefly the Emperor's Minister of Communications, amused himself by testing the limits of the credulity of French newspapers by making crazy claims. 'Bokassa wasn't an habitual cannibal,' Duchemin said. 'It is true that he kept human flesh in his fridge through politeness to or hospitality for certain of his fellow African heads of state. Of course, when one has an establishment like his to keep up, one thinks of one's guests. Like those people who don't like alcohol, but who nevertheless keep whisky, gin or Martini in their bar.'

Paris Match published a photo of two bodies in Bangui with a caption claiming that they were in the cold-room in the presidential palace, but in reality they were in the city's morgue. 'Is Bokassa a cannibal? asked *Paris Match*.

This was the question that the *Agence France Presse* asked after the discovery of four mutilated corpses were found packed in the refrigerator of one of the overthrown Emperor's residences. 'These bodies... were found in the villa Kolongo, at the exit of Bangui, on the road to Berengo [another of his residences]. Central Africans asked about this subject were unanimous: these cadavers, with arms and legs cut off, their viscera open, were destined for the personal consumption of the ex-dictator. Various testimony related persons who disappeared who would have been eaten by him at Berengo. The facts, according to this testimony, were known to all.'

As the author points out, much the same was said of Idi Amin Dada of Uganda.

Naturally, I was reminded of the time when I was contacted by lawyers to ask me whether, having visited Liberia during the civil war there, I had any information about the alleged cannibalism of Charles Taylor, the Libero-American who was then trying to overthrow the fragile government whose writ ran only in Monrovia, and subsequently became President of Liberia before he was hauled before the International Court of Justice and imprisoner for crimes against humanity. Taylor sued the academic, Stephen Ellis, who wrote a book on the Liberian civil war (infinitely better than mine), and also an article in the *Times*, alleging that he, Taylor, was a cannibal. Taylor decided to sue for libel and the *Times* was seeking witnesses who could justify the story. In the end, Taylor dropped the case because he would have had to appear in court in person and face cross-examination. There was an international warrant also for his arrest, but whether he feared the latter or the former more, I cannot say. But this was the first and last time I was ever considered as a possible witness in a trial over allegations of cannibalism.

Ceausescu was an interesting case. I happened to be in Romania three months before his, and his wife's, downfall. It is interesting that all six of the dictators chosen for the book were of humble origin and according to the author sought to erase memories of deprived childhoods by their extravagance as dictators, as if the present could eradicate or make different the past. Nevertheless, none of them developed a real taste for foreign cuisine, preferring the dishes that were familiar to them from their home regions, even if in their youth they were not able often to partake of them.

Communist regimes had a special line in food propaganda, extolling the huge quantities of comestibles produced under their solicitous direction. I well remember watching a television programme in my hotel in Romania about the phenomenal harvest that year of potatoes—one saw potatoes being piled up into something resembling the lesser Pyramids of Egypt. Outside on the street was a long line of people with shopping bags queuing for—potatoes.

Edmund Blunden was a First World War poet and memoirist, then Professor of English Literature at Tokyo and Hong Kong universities, and lastly Professor of Poetry at Oxford. He took a keen, not to say obsessive, interest in cricket, of which he was said to be an enthusiastic but bad player. He continued to write poetry prolifically until his death in 1979.

His collected poems written between 1930 and 1940, and published in 1940, has many poems harking back to that first war. Though the second had already started at the time the book was published, it had not yet become total, to judge by the book's physical quality. It is hardly surprising that the first war continued to haunt Blunden's imagination, for it was an experience that called forth one of two main responses: silence or continual remembrance. Blunden was of the remembrance party.

In *Near Albert-sur-Ancre, 1916,* Blunden recalls the ruined church:

> At the foot of the church tower I noticed some weeds…
> The church was a skeleton.

The final verse has a powerful image or images:

> It was one of those corners behind a great war
> Where nature had skulked like a spider or mouse,
> Appalled but persisting: just room and no more;
> Overlooked when the huge broom was sweeping the house.

In *War Cemetery* he asks:

> Why are they dead? Is Adam's seed so strong
> That these bold lives cut down mean nothing lost?

Death is, of course, the final destination of all of us, but:

> … though this dying business concerns
> The lot of us, there seems something amiss

When twenty million sudden funeral urns
Are called for. Have you no hypothesis?

Why this mass slaughter? In the war cemetery:

Dead lies my friend, the fighter, from whom I hardly
heard
Against a human enemy one unhumorous word.

Blunden must have been one of the very few poets to have
written an ode extolling Neville Chamberlain's efforts at
Munich. In a paean titled *Exorcized*, he expresses his relief that
peace in our time had been restored (it speaks to his honesty,
and to the freedom of the country, that he did not attempt to
excise this supposed exorcism even after the war had begun).
Blunden describes in the poem the nightmares to which a man
who had been through the first war is subject:

'My dreams,' said one, and spoke for all, 'less frequently
these nights recall
The clear-cut circumstances, the countless bitter facts
familiar then...'

It is not the memory of 'the dead in smashed-down den'
that haunts him, 'But that it is which shatter sleep, and makes
one's weary body leap... The War is on once more.'

But the Munich Agreement allays that fear:
The meeting of four men as friends unhorses all the
ancient fiends;

> Believing still to best will ever yield the best, and now it ends
> One swollen and final fear.

Blunden's horror of war—a horror that he had surely earned the right to feel and express—clouded his political judgment, and who could blame him? But Chamberlain, Hitler, Mussolini and Daladier friends, indeed! Neither Hitler nor Mussolini were men for friends or friendship, for they had no inner gifts to give. But if I had been alive at the end of 1938, I think I might well have been on the side of Appeasement, just for another year's, month's, day's peace. My judgment in such matters is no better than that of the average man.

Blunden wrote an elegy to Wilfred Owen, title *To W.O. and His Kind*. It is despairing about the prospect of war once more:

> If even you, so able and so keen,
> And marker of the business you reported,
> Seem now almost as though you had never been,
> And in your simple purpose nearly thwarted,
> What hope is there? What harvest from those hours
> Deliberately, and in the name of truth.
> Endured by you?

Blunden ends with a hopeless wish and an acknowledgement, perhaps, that he is not the equal of Owen:

> Would that you were not dust.
> With you I might invent, and make men try,
> Some genuine shelter from this frantic sky.

By one of those strange coincidences which must occur in a long life, I was rootling about among my books immediately after having read some of Blunden's poems, when I came across a slim volume of poems by another poet of the First World War, Edward Shanks. This book, simply called *Poems*, was published in 1916, at the height of the war. In it is an elegy, *The Dead Poet*, to Rupert Brooke, a very different kind of elegy from Blunden's to Owen:

> When I grow old they'll come to me and say:
> Did you then know him in that distant day?
> Did you speak with him, touch his hand, observe
> The proud eyes' fire, soft voice and light lips' curve?
> And I shall answer: This man was my friend;
> Call to my memory, add, improve, amend...

Shanks almost makes Brooke's early death seem like a benefit received—it sealed his reputation for ever—but foolish as it may seem, one knows what he, Shanks, means:

> Ah, pitiful
> The twisted memories of an ancient fool
> And sweet the silence of a young man dead!
> Now far in Lemnos sleeps that golden head,
> Unchanged, serene, for ever young and strong,
> Lifted above the chances that belong
> To us who live, for he shall not grow old,
> And only of his youth there shall be told
> Magical stories, true and wondrous tales,
> As of a god whose virtue never fails,

Whose limbs shall never waste, eyes never fail,
And whose clear brain shall not be dimmed at all.

How extraordinarily romantic, written at a time when 20,000 young men or more were being mown down daily before or not long after their age of majority! It's absurd, or wrong, or totally irrational, but yet we know what Shanks means and are moved by it. We tend to remember people as they last were, just before they died, not as the once were. This does not flatter us, those of us who live to be old. But of course, most of the young who died at Rupert Brooke's age of death leave nothing permanent behind to be remembered by, and therefore are soon forgotten.

Pace Edward Shanks, I think on the whole that death is best avoided, except where age or incurable illness is a terrible burden.

When I read in a newspaper that the novelist, Fay Weldon, had died, I felt a pang of guilt. I had met her only once and had thought she was a nice woman. Nevertheless, when she published a short story in an anthology to celebrate the fiftieth anniversary of the establishment of the National Health Service, a book that I had been asked to review, I described her story as sentimental claptrap. I have not read it again since, but I am reasonably certain that my judgment was correct and that the story *was* sentimental claptrap; but there was no need for me to have been so fierce in my criticism. She was, to my regret, hurt by it (I suppose I had thought that she would never get to see it), so hurt in fact that she communicated to me, by what means I now forget, that she knew who I was—I had written it under my pseudonym—and might reveal my identity, that at that time was still hidden, thus causing me professional embarrassment. She was not a person who deserved to be hurt: that is, if anyone deserves to be hurt. Now, after her death, I would never have the opportunity to apologise to her.

I suppose I was irritated at the time by the sentimental drivel that accompanied the anniversary, as if the NHS had been a tremendous, unparalleled and complete success, as if no medical treatment had existed before it, as if no other country had managed to treat patients as well as ours for lack of an NHS of their own, when it was quite clear that the performance of the NHS was, by international standards, mediocre at best, and quite possibly worse that mediocre. It was time for critical thought and reflection, and not for an orgy of self-congratulation.

Well, a popular novelist is not necessarily the person to look to for such critical reflection, especially not in a festschrift for a giant bureaucracy. I had met her at a conference on psychiatry and literature, at which she gave what would now, I suppose, be called a keynote speech. She taught me an interesting lesson in public speaking.

Her voice throughout was so quiet and subdued that one strained to make out what she was saying. One concentrated so hard on making out the words and was so delighted to be able to have done so, that one forgot altogether to think about their meaning in any critical fashion. It was a splendid way to deflect in advance all possible criticism. I assumed it was a deliberate and cunning ploy.

It was only many years later that, from a friend who knew her quite well, and who was himself not an uncritical type, that I learned that it was nothing of the sort. For physical reasons she could not raise her voice, and even in private she spoke very softly. I had not noticed this when I sat next to her at dinner after her talk: I had just supposed that she was talking confidentially to me, and I was flattered by it. But apparently there was something wrong with her vocal cords and she was quite unable to project her voice.

My friend who knew her said that she was indeed a very nice woman who, despite being a best-selling author, remained financially hard-up because she was so generous in her support of her family, who were much less successful than she. In fact, she came from a literary family, but that was no guarantee of prosperity. My friend, who appreciated her, was appalled when she revealed in her autobiography that when young she had prostituted herself. He said that, whether true or not, her taste had always been questionable. I asked him how he had first met her: it was through attendance at an Anglican church in the City.

My friend said that, notwithstanding his high regard for her as a person (and she had the face of a good person), he had never brought himself to read one of her books. He had started one but had given up after a few pages, it was so trashy. My friend's wife, who also knew her, but whom Fay Weldon considered hardly worth speaking to, found also that she could not read her books, suffused as they were with a militant feminism. Here was an irony! A feminist author who did not think a woman as worth talking to as a man, and a woman put off reading her by her feminism!

I, too, had never read any of her books, but just after her death came across one that sold for £0.99 in a charity shop. It was called *Worst Fears*. First published in 1996, it was in its fourth paperback printing by 1997. I don't know whether it is considered by aficionados to be one of her best novels, but among the blurbs on the back cover was that of the *Daily Mail*:

It is an extraordinary, discomforting, rage-spit of a novel.

The distinction between *discomfiting* and *discomforting* has largely been lost, but I had not previously heard the noun *rage-spit*. My vocabulary has been enlarged but not improved.

I thought the novel rather clever. If, finally, it did not quite cohere, I found it surprisingly worth the reading. Furthermore, it was not quite as trivial as I had expected it to be. Indeed, it could even be said, if one read it with indulgence, to raise important questions about the knowledge human beings can be said to have of one another.

The protagonist of the novel is an actress by the name of Alexandra Ludd who, as a feminist, insists on being called an *actor*: a development in verbal bullying that I should have put later than 1996. She and her husband have a cottage in a charming village, but she spends much time in London whenever she has a part on the stage. She is in London when her husband, a literary critic with a particular interest in Ibsen, dies of a heart attack. She is playing in *The Doll's House* when he dies. (She says of his book on Ibsen that it will soon be forgotten or superseded and will be found only on the shelves of old codgers—like me, one of those rare, shy creatures who likes superseded literary criticism.)

It is only after his death that she discovers how unfaithful her husband has been to her throughout their married life, not surprisingly a most unwelcome discovery. The book relates the twists and turns of her relations with the women in the village with whom he has been unfaithful, all of whom she thought she knew well.

Although Weldon was a feminist and portrays a man of no sexual scruple, it cannot be said that her women, at least in this book, are better than the male of the species.

What do we really know of each other, we humans? And would it always be better if we did know the truth?

Henry Drummond (1851-1897) was a Scottish scientist and missionary of the Free Church of Scotland who wrote a book, *Tropical Africa*, which was published in 1888, about his eight-month visit to Central Africa. Photographs of Drummond show him as pretty dour, perhaps as one might expect of someone for whom the prospect of Hell was always real, and admission thereto so very easy. These days, Christians are less keen on Hell than they used to be, as its existence does not consort well with a loving, kind God; but I must say that being sent for eternal torment always seemed to me excessive punishment for the wrongs that most men do, even when they do not repent of them.

Despite his rather grim expression, however, Drummond enjoyed life. He was alive to beauty and the one biographical study of his life said that 'There was a touch of the artist on his work; he never neglected the service of beauty so often and so painfully forgotten or ignored by many men of religious spirit and occupation... he had high spirits and a great appetite for fun.'[8]

Even if the camera of the time could not lie, it could certainly mislead.

My copy of Drummond's book (a best-seller in its day) is inscribed on the back of its beautiful pull-out map of Central Africa: *This book belongs to Paul Young who lives at Co-Op Butchary (sic) Linton Cambs*. The writing is childish and is another reminder that missionary literature was once a popular, or at least widespread, genre in the homes of children.

The map, which was very far from detailed, put me in mind of the verse of Jonathan Swift:

> So geographers in Afric maps
> With savage pictures fill their gaps,
> And o'er unhabitable downs
> Place elephants for want of towns.

There are no pictures on Drummond's map, but the names of tribes thought to inhabit blank stretches of land: the Ukonongo, the Uyanzi, the Ugogo, the Ukami, the Uzanamo, and so forth. A very large and indefinite area is marked GERMAN SPHERE OFF INFLUENCE. There are also marked British and Portuguese spheres of influence, though they are no more clearly delimited than the border between

---

[8] *The Practical Life and Work of Henry Drummond*, Cuthbert Lennox, New York, 1898, James Pott and company.

the Ukami and the Uzanamo.

There were two strings to Drummond's mental bow: science and religion. He believed in the blessings of both and sought to unite them. In his most famous book, approved of by no less a person than Mr Gladstone, *Natural Law in the Spiritual World*, Drummond reconciled the process of evolution with that of Divine Providence, the one being evidence of the other: *pace* the famous debate between T.H. Huxley and Bishop Wilberforce in Oxford, there was no contradiction between them. And this seems to me right, at least in the sense that it is no more difficult to believe than that Divine Providence works through human history: which is not the same, of course, as saying that Divine Providence actually exists. I don't believe that it does.

Drummond's interest in natural history is evident in *Tropical Africa*, for the longest chapter in the book is devoted to the biology of the white ant or termite, the enemy of the wood employed in permanent construction in Africa, but itself the builder of huge, almost cathedral-like structures in the bush. There is also an extensive chapter on insect mimicry, in which Drummond almost saw moral defect:

> However much the creatures impress you by their cleverness, you never quite get over the feeling that there is something underhand about it; something questionable and morally unsocial. The evolutionist also is apt to charge mimetic species in general with neglecting the harmonious development of their physical framework, and by cheap and ignoble subterfuge evading the appointed struggle for life. At the first revelation of all

these smart hypocrisies one is inclined to brand the whole system as cowardly and false.

The whole point of evolutionary theory is to account for change without resort to any conscious purpose: but we are beings whose minds are so imbued with purposiveness that we find it almost impossible to exclude purpose from our thoughts about anything. Even the most militant of evolutionists often says things like 'Evolution decreed that...' or 'Evolution required that...', as if evolution, or Evolution, were a purposive deity. About insect mimicry, the means by which a non-poisonous or harmless insect appears outwardly almost identical to a poisonous or dangerous one, Drummond goes on to ask:

> Is it nothing that, while in some animals the disguises tend to become more and more perfect, the faculties of penetrating them, in other animals, must continually increase in subtlety and power?

In other words, Drummond believes that the mimicry of potential prey sharpens the wits of potential predators such that, in a sense, there is progress.

Drummond believed in progress and thought that colonial enterprise and missionary activity would bring it: which it did if progress means a more complex material existence. He says that the Africans whom he encounters seem happy enough with their form of life but does not go on to ask why, then, they needed progress in his sense at all. He believed, naturally, that, being ignorant of the true faith, they needed religious enlightenment, but this has an implication not very flattering to the God who created them, in whom he believes, namely that He is willing to condemn sentient beings to eternal damnation merely for being ignorant through no fault of their own.

But Drummond is sympathetic towards the Africans. While he saw them as primitive in their current state, there is no implication in what he writes that they are inherently inferior or incapable, biologically as it were, of reaching the highest levels of cerebration. He is certainly not racist in that sense.

One of the curiosities of the book is the author's evident wish that the elephant be driven to complete extinction. The African elephant cannot be domesticated, or so it is said, or trained to any useful task—useful to humans, that is. Moreover, such was the market for ivory that it was at the root of the slave trade centred on the island of Zanzibar. The only effective way of suppressing that trade, therefore, according to Drummond, was to eliminate its motive, ultimately the elephant and its tusks. Of

> … half the real woes that now exist in Africa ivory is at the bottom. It is not only that wherever there is an article to which a fictitious value is attached the effect upon the producer is apt to be injurious; nor that wherever there is money there is temptation, covetousness, and war; but that unprincipled men, and especially Arabs, are brought into contact with the natives in the worst relation, influence them on only one, and that the lowest, direction, and leave them always worse than they find them—worse in greed, in knavery, in their belief in

mankind, and in their suspicion of civilisation. Further, for every tusk an Arab trader purchases, he must buy, borrow or steal a slave to carry it to the coast. The elephant has done much for Africa. The best he can now do for the country is to disappear for ever.

A long essay, perhaps even a book, taking in many contentious subjects, could be written taking this passage as an originating text.

A Scottish clergyman of similar ilk to Henry Drummond was John Cumming D.D (1807-1881). I had not heard of him until I came across a little book of his, published in 1854, in the most perfect condition, titled *Signs of the Times: The Moslem and His End, The Christian and His Hope*. The publisher was Arthur Hall, Virtue and Company, and I assumed that Virtue was a name rather than a self-attribution, as indeed it was. George Virtue lived from 1794 to 1868, and his partner, Arthur Hall, was active in the 1840s and 50s. Their company published mainly religious tracts, for which there was an almost infinite appetite then, to judge by the catalogue at the end of the book. It therefore took perspicacity on the part of Matthew Arnold, in the face of this deluge of tracts, to perceive at the time the long, melancholy withdrawing roar of religion in England.[9]

---

[9] The poem, *Dover Beach*, was most probably completed in 1851, though not published until 1867.

John Cumming ministered to a Scottish congregation in London for fifty years, besides which he was a prolific author of such works as *Infant Salvation: Or, All Saved Who Die in Infancy*, which is 'Specially addressed to Mothers mourning the loss of Infants and Children', a regrettably large class of person at the time; *Divine Dealing and Human Preparation*, which consists of 'Two sermons preached on the day of Humiliation, 1849', supposedly to ward off further outbreaks of cholera; and *Apocalyptic Sketches* in three volumes.

Cumming, like Drummond, appeared somewhat grim of countenance, the kind of man who did not know what men were doing when they laughed but knew that it was wrong.

He starts his little book with an orotund declaration:

> On all sides it seems to be felt that ours is no ordinary age. It is universally owned that we live in times of infinite importance.

A quarter of a century earlier, another Scotsman of prophetic inclinations, Thomas Carlyle, wrote a famous essay with the same title, *Signs of the Times*, in which he says, 'we too admit that the present is an important time,' but adds with an irony of which I suspect Cumming would have been incapable, 'as all present time necessarily is.' Two hundred years ago, Carlyle castigated what is now known as technocracy, namely the belief that, and conduct as if, all human problems were susceptible to a technical solution, whether it be social, constitutional or legislative. What of the inner man, cried Carlyle?

Cumming firmly believed that the world was 6000 years

old, not older, and that if one examined, or interpreted aright, the prophecies to be found in the Bible, the Second Coming [no pun intended] would be in 1864, or thereabouts (Carlyle mentioned the same prophecy, but with contempt).

Cumming's main claim to fame then as now—it is only a faint claim—was his fervent anti-Catholicism which he called the Western Apostasy, among other things, and referred to the Papacy as 'the Tiara'. He was also deeply opposed to the Church of England's tendency to Catholicism: 'Ignorant of vital and evangelical truth, it is occupied about robes, and candles, and genuflexions, and crosses, and phylacteries.' In my copy of the book is written in the margin of this passage the word *Shame!*, though whether the shame attached to the idolatry implied or the author's denunciation of it I cannot say. I suspect the former, for I also suspect that most of this type of book were bought and read by people who already agreed with them rather than by those who sought to learn something new. What is clear is that such questions still aroused great passion, questions that now seem to most of us trivial and all but incomprehensible. Matthew Arnold saw through this passion to the underlying loss of faith and the receding of the religious tide.

Cumming interprets the signs of the times through the Book of Revelation, with its mysterious seven vials, particularly the last of these. 'This vial,' he writes, 'let fall its first sprinklings, I believe, in 1848, and its influence still spreads. First, it is from that day to this on the fruits of the earth, from the vines of France, Spain and Madeira, to the potato of Ireland—a universal and destructive blight. Where is its birthplace? Medical men tell you, in the air. In vain, chemists analyse it;

in vain microscopes are applied; in vain it is assigned to a peculiarity of soil, season, climate, insects. The only ultimate explanation is the apocalyptic taint. The physical proof of the action of the seventh vial (of the wrath of God) is complete. But its effects are not confined to vegetable life. Cholera, a new and devastating pestilence existing like other diseases since the fall, but first seen here in 1832, as a premonition, came down upon England in 1849, and ere it ceased, I recollect—for I was in the midst of it—three thousand per week were gathered to their graves. No theory explains this; no material skill has penetrated its secret.'

As it happens, 1854, the year of the publication of this book, was also the year in which Dr John Snow, a brilliant pioneer of anaesthesia as of epidemiology, demonstrated the transmission of cholera by water, one of the first triumphs of the latter science. From the point of view of timing, Cumming's book could hardly have been worse.

Cumming continues: 'Poverty, filth, bad drainage, crowded hovels, long hours in unventilated shops, do not create it [cholera]; but they draw it close, as iron conductors draw down lightning; and they nurse, and feed, and strengthen it, till it goes forth from the hovels of the poor to the halls of the great, conquering and to conquer, with terrible and disastrous success... I look at cholera less as the gift of God—more as a retribution for the sins and misdoings of mankind.'

The political situation is also a sign of the approaching Second Coming 'The same prophetic record that thus indicates the near downfall of Mahometanism, informs us that this downfall is to make way for the march of "kings from the sun-rising." Whether this refers to the Jews[10], as I believe, or to the emergence of the ancient Oriental Church, is a matter of dispute. But this is certain, that the Christians of the East will gain in all respects by the winning of the Crescent.'

Cumming believed that Turkey, or the Ottoman Empire, was in terminal decline, and that this meant that it would take Islam down with it. From the present standpoint—who can say from that of a hundred years hence—nothing could have been more erroneous.

But since Turkey is destined to be annihilated as a power, it is right for Britain and France to defend it for the moment because there is worse: 'I believe that the war now provoked by the ambition of the Russian Autocrat, and accepted by our country, is a war not only of policy, but of justice, of truthfulness, of mercy. The guilt rests on Russia. I pity the infatuated Autocrat; may his punishment be signal[11], or his repentance speedy! May his ambition meet with reward! May he learn in the Kremlin that justice and truth and mercy are stronger than the Cossacks, and more enduring than armed battalions.'

At the present conjuncture, this is an interesting passage. Cumming says:

> We have no sympathy with the Koran, no desire to uphold the Mosque, no wish to see the Osmanli strike deeper, or extend wider his withering footprint. But we have no less dread of autocratic tyranny, and of the lust

---

[10] Cumming was a strong Zionist *avant la lettre*.

[11] Nicholas I did indeed die during the war.

of power. Acquiescence in this matter would be connivance. It would not ultimately avert war.

In my late adolescence, the theatre flourished in London, possibly as never before (or since). The standard of acting and productions was very high, and the intelligence of the plays performed much higher than it is now. Even if there were more subsidies then than there are now, there was evidently a large audience for serious plays (I don't exclude comedies from seriousness). Even in the provinces the standard was high: new plays were tried out in Birmingham, Manchester and Nottingham. I don't know whether it is a true correlation, but it seems that there was a larger appetite for good theatre before the great expansion of tertiary education.

I remember Alec McCowen in Peter Luke's play, *Hadrian VII*. It was given first, to great applause, at the Birmingham Repertory Theatre before moving to London, where I saw it. Of course, the play was largely an adaptation of Frederick Rolfe's novel, *Hadrian the Seventh*. As far as I know, Peter Luke never wrote as successful a play again, though his career as a television dramatist was not entirely unsuccessful. But nothing of his sticks in the mind as does his *Hadrian VII*. Of the play, the theatre critic, Harold Hobson (once a name to conjure with, now forgotten to literature), said '[Hadrian VII] appeals to extremely powerful elements in human nature. Everyone who feels in himself the presence of extraordinary abilities which an envious world has failed to recognize… will find that this splendid, colourful, recklessly melodramatic and vituperatively brilliant drama speaks to him in irresistible tones.' In other words, one might add, the play is a study of one of the prevailing emotions of our times (perhaps of all times), namely resentment.

Hadrian VII is the story of a peculiar man unable to distinguish very clearly fantasy from reality. He ardently desires to be ordained a priest of the Catholic church, but is thwarted for many years on pretexts, or what he believes to be pretexts, of his unsuitability and lack of vocation for the priesthood, past misdemeanours, and so forth. Yet throughout all his disappointment, he retains his ardour, and being both intelligent and of a scholarly disposition, becomes an expert on aspects of church history. Eventually, however, he is granted holy orders: and because of an impasse in the choice of a new Pope after the death of Leo XIII[12,] he, Frederick Rolfe, the self-styled Baron Corvo, is raised to the papacy as Hadrian VII. The difference between dream and reality is dissolved.

During his imagined papacy, Hadrian VII seeks to return the church to its evangelical purity, renouncing both temporal sovereignty and its great treasures. Cardinal Pagna, the Vatican's hardnosed Secretary of State, is at first horrified, but comes to see Hadrian as a saint and divinely inspired. At no point does he object that the abandonment of the church's treasures would be a philistine thing to do. Whether to do so is good or bad is measured by the sole yardstick of holiness, of its compatibility with or observance of Christ's teaching. The

---

[12] He died in 1903. Rolfe published his book the following year.

good of civilisation doesn't come into it, just as it doesn't come into the consideration of the young fanatics who glue themselves to painting or throw soup at them, ostensibly to save the planet. The church is preserved from Hadrian's philistinism only by his assassination or martyrdom at the hand of an Irish Protestant fanatic.

The play both opens and closes with Rolfe in his cold and uncomfortable garret dunned for money by bailiffs. All that has occurred in between—his ordination and elevation to the papacy—is but fantasy, that of an embittered man taking his revenge in his imagination on reality for all the wrongs and humiliations that he has suffered. That he invited his own humiliations does not really occur to him: he is acerbic and arrogant in his dealings with those who might otherwise help him, making it perfectly clear that he regards himself as their superior. A real careerist would, of course, be more emollient and compromising, at least until he were in a position to act on his accumulated resentment—probably unassuageable. Rolfe sabotages the very ascent he believes himself to merit and to which he believes himself entitled.

This is far from uncommon in human reality—Hobson was right. The commonest reason for self-sabotage, I surmise, is that the person who indulges in it wants a reason or excuse in advance for the failure that he foresees. He fears that, in a truly just world, he would still fail and would be unable to account for his failure other than by his own incapacity. This self-sabotage is a beguiling tactic for those who are ambitious but suspect that they are not, as the French say, *à la hauteur*: not up to it, as we say, rather less elegantly.

Personally, I am more comfortable with failure than with

success, being of course more familiar with it—failure, that is, of a certain kind: I am not talking of park-bench alcoholics.[13] No; I speak of gifted persons who have some defect or other (in this context, lack of singlemindedness or ruthlessness counts as a defect) that prevents them from succeeding when all else might conduce to success: a man, for example, who writes but hesitates to put what he has written before an editor or a publisher, let alone the public, because of what, in religious terms, would be termed *scruple*. Yet perhaps this is rationalisation to prevent him from coming face to face with his own feared lack of talent. He has looked into his soul and found it not as deep as he had hoped.

This, naturally, brings me to my own preference for failures. One can always measure up to failure. Not a few clever people whom I have known preferred to surround themselves with mediocrities, and powerful politicians do the same. I am aware of this failing in myself: at any rate I am content to spend much of my time with people who, while far from stupid, I know will not criticise my writing.

I know nothing of the life or character of Peter Luke, but I wonder whether it was the presence in him of something akin to Hadrian VII that enabled him to write his one very powerful play for the stage, and in the end to be remembered for nothing else? Is it enough in a life to have written one admired play, if your ambition was to have been to be a great writer? To have written one such play is more than most writers achieve, but it is thin gruel for a large appetite.

As for great successes in life, either in their own estimate or

---

[13] Though they may have their tragic and affecting stories.

in that of others, they both intimidate and appal me. They seem to progress on well-oiled wheels, not on the crutches that most of us use. They charge ahead, they achieve, they do not look back (or have to), they do not ruminate about or regret what might have been. And yet I do not envy them, not one hundred per cent.

In his introduction to a collection of essays titled *A Writer's Nightmare*, the great Indian writer, R.K. Narayan, says that his father used to read such writers as Macaulay, Carlyle and Froude. Narayan junior found them hard-going, and preferred personal, discursive essays such as those by Charles Lamb or Robert Lynd (it came as a surprise to me to see the second mentioned because I thought that by 1988, when the book was published, Lynd had been entirely, if unjustly, forgotten).

Narayan says that the personal, discursive essay has gone out of fashion (well before the advent of the internet), but that for twenty years he had written such an essay weekly for the newspaper, *The Hindu*. He did so not because he always had something urgent to say, but because he needed an income. The three novels he had written when he started had brought him more esteem than money, which he then badly needed. And no one but a blockhead, said Doctor Johnson, ever wrote, except for money.

Narayan is of an India that I remember from my visits there (for the first time in 1969). I haven't been back for some years, and I suspect that the country's headlong economic development is fast destroying the India that I knew and liked so much. I am sure that life for many millions, who have been lifted from abject poverty, has improved greatly, but I also cannot help feeling that something must have been lost as well, namely a subtlety, a sense of humour, an absence of vulgarity, that I found so attractive. When I attended the wedding of the nephew of a friend of mine in Calcutta (the young man is now a judge), I asked my friend's brother, now alas deceased, the meaning of the Sanskrit prayers that the pandit, seated round a small sacred fire, was intoning as he fed the fire with sandalwood. 'I don't know,' he replied, 'it's all Greek to me.'

Such irony suffused Narayan's writing which, I fear, is going the way of the discursive essay in public taste. Headlong improvement is not propitious to irony.

One of the essays in the book is about Narayan's time as a visiting professor at a Mid-Western university in the United States. Narayan wondered what a visiting professor was supposed to do, and no one could tell him. I have known visiting professors who have styled themselves 'professor' ever afterwards, though with the ever-growing profusion of both chairs and academic subjects, the title has been devalued, as precious metal coins were once clipped. In my day (O, fatal phrase!) professors were very few and mostly distinguished for something, including scholarship. Now the title does not distinguish between scholar, bureaucrat and careerist.

In the Mid-West of those days, an Indian was thought to be, *ex officio*, in tune with mystical forces. Everyone assumed Narayan to be some kind of guru. He recounts an hilarious episode:

A senior professor of the English department approached me once to ask I would meet her students. I agreed, since that was the purpose of my sojourn on the campus. Nearer the time of the actual engagement, I met her again to work out the details.

'What am I expected to do in your class?' I asked.

She replied promptly. 'My students want to hear you on Indian mysticism.'

I told her point blank, 'I know nothing about it.'

'That shouldn't matter at all,' she said.

'Of course it matters a great deal to me. When I go to a class I should like to speak on a subject which I know or at least have the pretence of knowing. I do not want to parade my ignorance in a classroom.'

She seemed to think that it was an extraordinary piece of diffidence on my part and said encouragingly, 'Please, half-an-hour will be enough. You can tell them anything you like about mysticism, just for thirty minutes.'

'Not even for half-a-minute. Why did you commit me to this engagement?'

Her answer was startling. 'Because they have demanded it. They want you to talk on Indian mysticism.'

The essay is undated, but I should imagine that it comes from the era of the Beatles' mysticism: that is to say, from more than fifty years ago. Thus, the ruination of higher education is not of recent date, unless fifty years be counted of recent date. It depends, I suppose, on your time perspective.

The anecdote reminds me of an occasion when the *Daily Mail* called me at about two in the afternoon and asked me whether I could write a thousand[14] on 'this new cancer treatment' by four o'clock. I said that I couldn't, for two reasons: first, I was in outpatients, and second, I knew nothing about it.

There was a silence for a moment from the other end of the phone.

'All right, then,' came the reply, 'four-thirty.'

Thus are the public informed.

The same newspaper once called me and asked whether I could go to India the day after next. Naturally, I enquired why.

'It's the Kumbh Mela,' they said.

They explained to me that the Kumbh Mela was a Hindu festival held every twelve years when the Ganges at Allahabad is believed to change, spiritually rather than materially, into an ambrosia that washes away sins. Every twelfth Kumbh Mela is an especially propitious one, and this year's Kumbh Mela was this special one. Ninety million people were expected to attend.

'Let's get this right,' I said. 'You've had a hundred-and-forty-four years' notice of this event and you want me to go to India the day after tomorrow. Couldn't you have given me a bit more notice?'

'We don't work like that, Theo,' they said.

'Evidently not.'

But I went all the same and am eternally grateful to the newspaper for having sent me on a day-trip to India. The Kumbh Mela was far the most wonderful event I have ever

---

[14] A thousand words.

attended, with sadhus who had held their arms aloft so long, thirty years and more, that they were completely ankylosed, fortune-telling sparrows, Californian gurus in saffron robes and with chunky gold rings, brilliantly decorated cows, and millions on millions of pilgrims of every type and condition, the whole peacefully and joyfully assembled.

What was the nightmare of Narayan's title? That of having to produce copy every week irrespective of whether the writer had anything to say? No: the title refers to a nightmare that he had had. The government had printed five million forms for the official controller of stores, but the last word was misprinted as *stories*, and rather than let the forms go to waste had decided to set up a department for the control of stories.

The article is hilarious: it is pointed without bitterness. But absence of bitterness has gone out of fashion as much as have discursive essays.

On the negative recommendation of R.K. Narayan, I turned to the essay by James Anthony Froude, *Times of Erasmus and Luther*, that Narayan found such hard going. As it happened, I possessed the two volumes of Froude's *Short Studies on Great Subjects*, in which it appears in book form. My edition, dating from 1872, three years after the first, is handsomely bound, and has a very neat handwritten dedication in Latin:

Joanni Bain
Ob literas Graecas et Latinas feliciter excultas dedit
Edmundus D.A. Morshead

which means, I think:

John Bain
For the Greek and Latin letters were successful
Edmund D.A. Morshead

The latter was a Victorian schoolmaster at Winchester who was celebrated for his translations of Aeschylus into old-fashioned English verse. Was John Bain, I wonder, the son of Alexander Bain, the Scottish professor of philosophy and founder of the journal, *Mind*?

I didn't find Froude's essay, which started life as three public lectures delivered in Newcastle-upon-Tyne (I doubt that he would find an audience there today on any subject whatever), difficult in any way. I imagine that what Narayan found difficult, and actually offensive, was Froude's assumption that the history of Europe, and only part of Europe at that, was the whole of human history, as if India, China, Persia, etc., had no histories of their own. Probably Froude did not know, or did not care, that the population and economic product of both China and India of the time of which he wrote exceeded that of Europe by far.

Anglicised in many ways as Narayan was (a stamp issued by India to commemorate him showed a boy in the background playing cricket), he would not have grown up with the division between Protestant and Catholic running in his veins, as it were. Disputes over Christian doctrine would have seemed arcane and meaningless to him, and probably utterly mysterious, but for the minimally educated European, Froude's essay on the difference between Erasmus and Luther would be perfectly comprehensible and possibly still pregnant with meaning. The fact is that Froude was a good writer—by good I mean one who can still be read with pleasure for his style alone. I presume that it was for this that Narayan's father so admired him, rather than for the content or subject matter of what he wrote.

A good style, however, is not the same as solidity of scholarship. In my copy of the essay, I found inserted a yellowing little piece of newsprint, a letter to *The Times*:

> Sir,—A letter which you publish today contains the statement, 'Ignatius Loyola is said to have laid down the New Testament hastily, saying that he cherished his devotional feelings.' It is true, as your correspondent avers, that this has been said; but the sayer of it was the late Mr J.A. Froude, and it is one of these assertions of the thing that is not which disfigured nigh every page of that brilliant writer. In correction of it, may I be permitted to point out before your readers the following extract from my work, Renaissance Types (p. 146)?

The letter is signed W.S. Lilley, a barrister and historian who converted to Catholicism, and whose book was published in 1901. The letter, therefore, must be subsequent to that date, but before 1919, when he died.

Assuming Froude to have been a careless or even mendacious scholar, does that mean that he is not worth reading today? After all, why should we read an author whose every page contains a falsehood, that is to say, in the words of W.S. Lilley, a 'thing that is not'?

I read the essay on the tram from Wolverhampton to Birmingham and on the way back, in the presence of Saturday night drunks one of whom tried to sit on top of another. I read it with pleasure, though whether with instruction is another matter.

Froude was not favourable to Catholicism, or at least to what it had become by the time of Erasmus and Luther (and in the condition in which he believed that it had remained), but he is not a fanatic or bigot of the deep-dyed kind. He says:

> Imagine, if you can, a person now being put to death for a speculative theological opinion. You feel at once that in the most bigoted country in the world such a thing has become impossible; and the impossibility is the measure of the alteration we have all undergone.

This is interesting for two reasons, bearing in mind that it was written more than 150 years ago. First it is, if true, a sign of moral progress. Second, it implies that Matthew Arnold's long, melancholy withdrawing roar of religion, spotted by him a good many years before, was real. If we are not prepared to kill one another (or to die) for our religious beliefs, they are no longer all-in-all to us.

But is it true that we can no longer imagine a person being put to death for a speculative theological opinion? Alas, it is not true, or it has of late become less true. Christians no longer believe in their doctrines with the certainty to put people to death for denying them, but this is not true of Islamic doctrine in some Islamic countries. But religion for Froude meant Christianity in its major forms (though he does not mention

Orthodoxy): other religions are below his mental radar.

He understands the danger of making opinion the touchstone of virtue. 'Obedience to the law,' he says, 'is dispensed with if men will diligently profess certain opinions, or punctually perform certain external duties. However scandalous the moral life, the participation of a particular rite, or the profession of a particular belief... is held to clear the score.' This, I fear, may describe our moral atmosphere today.

Against this, Froude clearly prefers Luther to Erasmus. He concedes that the latter was a brilliant scholar, abstractly wise, who to preserve the peace was willing to go back on principles. Anything, in short, for a quiet life. Luther, by contrast, is *pur et dur* in the cause of Truth and obedience to God's Law. And yet, at the same time, Froude admits that:

> ... there is no proof, such as will satisfy the scientific inquirer, that there is any such thing as moral truth—any such thing as absolute right and wrong at all.

This, of course, makes Lutheran certainty untenable, at least intellectually, and yet he prefers it to Erasmus's trimming and acceptance of life as it is. These problems and contradictions are still with us, and make Froude still worth the reading, even if his scholarship is doubtful.

In what I rather grandly, but not altogether inaccurately, call *my library*, there is a curiosity with the title *Although He Was Black*, by a children's author called Lucy Laing. It was first published exactly a hundred years ago as I write this, though my edition, as far as I can tell the second and last, dates from some time in the 1930s. My copy was awarded to Neil Radcliffe as a prize in 1944 by a Baptist church in Leeds. It was printed by the mainstream publisher, Thomas Nelson and Company.

The story, aimed, I should imagine, at children of eight or nine, tells how a father, Mr Dorrell, returns home from America after a long time away, his two sons, Tom and Hugh, having in the meantime been looked after by a maiden aunt, Miss Dorrell. Today, we should assume that Mr Dorrell was separated or divorced from the children's mother, but when Lucy Laing wrote, readers would have assumed that Mrs Dorrell had died.[15]

Mr Dorrell has brought a surprise home for his sons. Is it a money or a parrot, they ask excitedly? No, it turns out to be a little black boy, an orphan called Sambo, who refers to himself as *dis nigger*. In the mouth of a white person, even then, the word *nigger* was derogatory, if not an outright insult. When the family chauffeur called John first comes across Sambo, he exclaims, 'My word! *I* don't know what we are going to do with a dirty nigger about the place.'

Sambo took the slight 'with a calm, beneficent smile,' but Hugh said, 'Oh no, he is not *dirty*; don't say that please, John. He can't help being black; and you do wash yourself, don't you. Sambo?'

This put me in mind of when—more than fifty years ago—

---

[15] Lucy Laing's last book, as far as I have been able to ascertain, was published in 1951, when the same assumption would have been made.

some student friends and I hired a gypsy caravan and horse for a couple of weeks to tramp round the lanes of County Cork. One of us was a young Ethiopian medical student, a most remarkable young man. He had been a shepherd and goatherd before he had won a scholarship to Uppingham School. (He had a photograph of himself shaking hands with Haile Selassie on the presentation of the scholarship, funded by an English friend of Ethiopia, which impressed us deeply.) Walking through an isolated village where no black man had ever set foot, he was approached by a small boy who ran his finger down his cheek and looked at its pulp to see whether the black had come off. This was curiosity, not malice.

Sambo had saved Mr Dorrell's life in America by rescuing him when he had a cramp while swimming. Mr Dorrell enjoins his children to be nice to Sambo, and they become his firm friends, though he remains, for the time being, a servant. John, the chauffeur, is by contrast cruel to him and one day, in a state of inebriation, throws a bottle at him and injures him. The coach house, where both John and Sambo are lodged, catches fire, and Sambo, having fainted, is buried in the cinders. He is rescued, however, but one of his arms has been crushed and has to be amputated.

John has been dismissed as an alcoholic, but sometime later returns in disguise and meets Sambo again. By this time he, John, has tuberculosis—not an unlikely fate for an alcoholic in 1924—and a little while later is admitted to hospital to die. He calls Sambo to his deathbed to ask for his forgiveness, which Sambo freely accords him, and Sambo is later surprised to have been left £500 in cash in John's will, a very large sum in those days, which Sambo uses to obtain the education he has always wanted. Having obtained a university degree, he sets sail to teach at the British School in Rio de Janeiro. The Dorrell children have remained his close friends and wave him off. Tom Dorell says (these are the last words of the book), 'Dear old chap, he was one of the whitest fellows I ever know—although he was black.'

Certainly, no one could, or would, write such a story today. The very name *Sambo* is a stereotype, and there is a great deal of condescension in the idea that being white is the greatest compliment that anyone could pay (Harree Jamset Ram Singh, the Indian schoolboy of Franck Richards' *Billy Bunter* stories was said to be 'a white man deep inside'—though in fact Frank Richards was resolutely opposed to racism when it was not reprehended as it is now, and makes the Indian easily the most intelligent of his schoolboy chums).

But Lucy Laing's story, ludicrous and demeaning as it appears to us now, was not racist in the sense that it displayed hostility to blacks as such or that it considered them in any way inferior. Sambo is the hero of the story and shows himself physically brave, morally admirable and mentally capable, obtaining a university degree as soon as the opportunity presented itself to him.

Still, the title now jars—*Although He Was Black*—and I doubt that anyone would now trouble to read it before denouncing it.

In William Blake's *Songs of Innocence*, written a hundred and thirty years earlier, there is a sentiment not dissimilar to that expressed in Lucy Laing's book:

My mother bore me in the southern wild,

And I am black, but O my soul is white!

These are the opening lines of the poem, *The Little Black Boy*. No one could seriously think that Blake was a racist, notwithstanding a verse such as the following, put into the mouth of the Little Black Boy:

And we are put on earth a little space,
That we may learn to bear the beams of love;
And these black bodies and the sunburn face
Are but a cloud and like a shady grove.

That cloud, says Blake through the words of the mother, will vanish, and there will be no difference between black and white.

The modern inquisitors of race and racism would no doubt find a *casus belli* against Blake in this poem. Why a little black boy as the marker of difference and not a little white one? (Never mind that Blake lived all his life among in an overwhelmingly white population, in which a black would have been only less exotic than a white in Timbuktu.) Why should whiteness of soul be considered the acme of goodness etc. etc? Plenty of reasons, then, to attach trigger warnings to this poem, and by extension to *all* his poetry.

It is wrong, then, to be touched by *The Fly*. Strange to relate, I cannot see a fly on a windowpane, provided it is not one of many, without thinking of it:

Little Fly,
Thy summer's play

My thoughtless hand
Has brushed away.

Am I not
A fly like thee?
Or art thou not
A man like me?

For I dance,
And drink and sing,
Till some blind hand
Shall brush my wing.

Without going quite to the extent of Jains[16], does this not teach a reverence for life itself?

Of course, I feel quite differently about flies *en masse*, for example those that pullulate around carrion. But then I also feel differently about men in particular and men in the mass.

Although as many as a third or a half the number of people died in the Burundian Civil War as in the Rwandan genocide of 1994, I have only one book about Burundi for ever twenty that I have about Rwanda. Perhaps this is because the civil war lasted thirteen years, the Rwandan genocide for three months. The former did not lack for genocidal intent, but the

---

[16] Orthodox Jains go to lengths not to harm insects. Unfortunately, such benevolence is not always reciprocated.

genocide was in the hands of gangs rather than that of the government. Who says that private initiative is always more efficient?

My brother-in-law gave me a copy of a novel about, or at least set largely, in Burundi, *Petit pays* (Small Country) by Gaël Faye. It came with his recommendation, but I long resisted reading it because of the little biography of the author that said that he has been influenced by hip-hop culture. So great is my contempt for this culture that I found it difficult to believe that anyone who could be influenced by it, or even claim to be so, could write something worthwhile (I once knew a promising young African writer who suddenly grew enamoured of hip-hop and nothing was ever heard of him again).

However, in this case at least I was quite mistaken. (It is sometimes a pleasure to own up to a mistake, for it lends credence that one's other judgments are not the product of pure prejudice and that one has not become mentally rigid.) *Petit pays* was indeed a short and powerful semi-autobiographical novel with both lyrical and dramatic aspects, very well fused.

The author is the son of a French father and Rwandan mother, the latter of whom took refuge in Burundi to escape one of the periodic massacres of Tutsi that preceded the intended final genocide, and that, though horrific enough, did not approach the latter in size or thoroughness. The protagonist, Gabriel or Gaby for short, grows up in a relatively privileged quarter of the capital, Bujumbura, where his father tries to protect him from the toxic politics and undercurrent of vicious ethnic hatred in the country. Gaby spends his childhood in a tiny country of his own within the little country (as, of course, many of us do).

I was briefly in Bujumbura seven years before the outbreak of the civil war. I went to the American embassy seeking information about the current political situation and was told by the press attaché that Burundi had so modernised and developed economically that it had put ethnic antagonism behind it. A drunk Belgian in a bar (Burundi had been mandated to Belgium after the First World War, having briefly been held by the Germans) had told me the evening before that, as far as he was concerned, 'the tall ones' (the Tutsi) were much better than 'the short ones' (the Hutu), and that they still hated one another. As a prognosticator, the drunk Belgian was far better than the American press attaché, though one never knows whether the latter type of person says what he believes to be true, or what he has been told to say. Sometimes, in my more naïve moments, I have thought that the life of a diplomat—a man sent abroad to lie for his country—must be very agreeable, one of comfort and cocktail parties: but on the contrary, never being allowed to speak in your own voice, except in the strictest privacy, must be a kind of torture—or so, at least, it would be for me.

Gaby's parents argue a lot and finally break apart. The family is, as is known, a little empire with its revolutions, and what happened in Gaby's family soon happened in the whole country. But even as the situation deteriorates, Gaby's world remains a tiny and protected one, his life at school and his friendships and childish enmities, completely centred on the *impasse*, or cul-de-sac, in which he lives with his father.

How many of the scenes in this book brought back to me

memory, or memories, of my own time in Africa! Every month, Gaby's father and Gaby visit Jacques, who lives in what was then still, under Mobutu's rule, Zaire. They cross the border from Burundi into Zaire: 'Immediately after the border-post, we changed world. Burundian restraint gave way to Zairean tumult.' This is exactly how I remember it: on the Rwandan side order, on the Zairean side chaos. Order and efficiency are not necessarily a good thing, of course, if you are planning a genocide:

> In a rusty sentry-box, a drowsy soldier weakly waved a fly- whisk. The diesel fumes mixed with the hot air dried the gullet of the government official, who had not been paid for a month. On the roads, immense craters which had formed where there had been potholes damaged the cars. But that did not at all prevent the customs official from meticulously inspecting each car, verifying the condition of the tyres, the level of the water in the engine, and the proper working of the indicators. If the vehicle revealed none of the hoped-for defects, the customs officer demanded the baptismal or first communion certificate for permission to enter the country.

It had taken me ten days to obtain my visa to enter Zaire. The consulate at Dar-es-Salaam, though officially open, had no staff in it until I was able fleetingly to catch one after ten days. Of course, he made out that stamping my passport was a labour of Herculean difficulty; but I have to admit that for sheer difficulty on my way across Africa by public transport, the border between Rwanda and Zaire did not present the most obstacles. That dubious honour went to the border between Niger and Mali, where it took the packed little bus in which I was travelling three days and nights to progress a hundred yards because the frontier guards, the customs men and the soldiers (on the Malian side) demanded to be paid by the passengers. Some of the prisoners were imprisoned until they paid up; the rest, as did I, had to sleep under the stars by the side of the road. When, after three days, I lost my patience and complained, shouting *Pots de vin! Pote de vin! Pots de vin!*— Bribes! Bribes! Bribes!—a soldier said to me, not unkindly, 'Remember, monsieur, that we have not been paid for three months.' I felt ashamed of my little fit of temper, which none of the other passengers had shown.

Nothing that Gaby recounts is exaggerated. On the laterite road from the Rwandan border to Kisangani, then little more than a track, not only were there immense crevices, but the local villagers dug deep elephant traps for vehicles to fall into, charging the owners for their services to extract them. The only sane response was laughter—and patience. I do not remember any moral outrage at this behaviour.

Jacques is what used to be known as an *African retread*, a tyre that has been punctured and repaired many times for lack of new tyres, in other words an African colonial who could never adjust to life anywhere else. He complains of his African servants though he could not do without them and even feels affection for them as he is insulting them:

> My macaque [monkey] in the kitchen burns everything under the pretence that it kills parasites. I don't know any longer what a good rare steak is. I can't wait to return to

121

Brussels for the treatment of my dysentery!

This is exactly how such people speak—or once spoke, perhaps they no longer exist.

The story of the book, dramatic and tragic, is convincing. One small detail recalled to me my brief time in Zimbabwe (then Rhodesia). At the sudden seasonal appearance of the flying ants, which lasted only a day or two, all activity came to a halt while this great delicacy was gathered by every able-bodied person for a God-given feast.

In Ismail Kadare's novel about his time as a student at Moscow's Gorky Institute, the most prestigious literary institute in the Soviet Union, he mentions, not very favourably, a Soviet literary critic, Vladimir Yermilov (Ermilov in the French transcription). In a way, Kadare was lucky in the timing of his studies: the Albania of Enver Hoxha was on the verge of falling out terminally with the Soviet Union of Nikita Khruschev, which meant the Kadare was able subsequently to write frankly, truthfully and disobligingly about the country, warts and all. Had he studied earlier, when the Soviet Union was still supposed to be the bastion of Leninist correctitude and a beacon to the world, he would not have been able to publish his novel.

Yermilov was still a prominent literary critic when Kadare was there, but he had not many more years to live, dying in 1965, four years after Kadare's departure. I don't suppose his name would mean much to a western reader today (or even when Kadare's novel was first published outside Albania in 1981) but it meant a little something to me because, more than half a century ago, I bought and read Yermilov's book on Chekhov, published by Progress Publishers of Moscow without date appended. Since I never throw out a book, however bad, I have it still: and to my great pleasure, I was able, more than fifty years later, to put my hand straight on it.

I now remember little of it, except that Yermilov made an attempt—it seemed to me at the time quite a good attempt—to turn Chekhov into a forerunner of the Bolshevik Revolution. Of course, this was preposterous, for no man was ever more averse to the reduction of life to an ideology, or even a philosophy, than Chekhov. But it was obligatory at the time in the Soviet Union to see all great Russian writers (with the exception, perhaps, of Dostoyevsky, who was not much printed or written about) as forerunners of the Revolution. And Yermilov had a long history of bending to the obligatory.

It is said that Yermilov played an important part in provoking the suicide of Mayakovsky, the pro-revolutionary poet, in 1930, but I am not sure that this is correct. Mayakovsky, who had always been granted an exit visa for his visits to Paris, was suddenly refused one and in the circumstances of the time, this refusal could be taken as the writing on the wall as far as his future was concerned. Perhaps he preferred to end his days rather than have them ended for him.

Nevertheless, Yermilov had joined the baying pack of critics that had accused Mayakovsky of literary unorthodoxy, namely modernism, a crime with an often-fatal outcome. During the 1920s, the Russian Association of Proletarian

Writers (RAPP) was in the literary ascendent, and Yermilov adhered to it. The wheel of ideological fortune turned, however, and the association was abolished. Some of its members, Leopold Averbakh for example, were executed; another member, Alexander Fadeyev, committed suicide.

Yermilov, however, managed to survive and prosper. His literary specialty was in the denunciation of other writers, a hazardous specialty because it was necessary to denounce not only the right person, but the right person at the right time. This required talent of a kind, the literary equivalent of insects' antennae.

Kadare spent some time in a rest-home on the Baltic with other writers, among whom Yermilov was one. His reaction to him was of repugnance:

> I remember the florid countenance of the critic, Yermilov, which was odious to me because I knew that he was one of those responsible for Mayakovsky's suicide. Every time I saw him, small and ugly, having lunch in the rest-home's dining room, I was astonished that all the writers did not pounce on him to hit him, lynch him, drag him along the road, on the sand dunes and up to the fountains of the sculpted dolphins. And from time to time, I said to myself: As long as that does not happen, it means that there is something not right in this rest-home, which is the opposite of what it should be.

A couple of days later, Kadare says, 'I passed the fountains of the sculpted dolphins, where I ought to have killed Yermilov long ago.' As V.S. Naipaul said of the Ayatollah

Khomeini's fatwa on Salman Rushdie, this is literary criticism of unusual severity. Of course, Kadare offered Yermilov no violence.

Turning to Yermilov's book on Chekhov, published in English after Kadare's departure from the Soviet Union, one moves from denunciation to near eulogy. The book was translated by Ivy Litvinov, British wife of the former Soviet foreign minister, Maxim Litvinov, whom Ivy Low married when he was a revolutionary plotter in London in 1916. That both she and her husband survived the Stalin purges has been called a miracle.[17] Ivy lived most of her adult life in the Soviet Union but returned to England for the last five years of her life, dying aged 88 in Hove, where many people go to die after vegetating. She translated not only Chekhov but Yermilov's book about him, as well as other classic Russian authors, and in 1930 wrote a crime novel set in Moscow and, much later, a book of short stories first published in the *New Yorker*. She also published two novels before she ever met Litvinov. She was obviously a formidable personage.

Yermilov's book is part biographical and part critical. He starts by describing Chekhov's antecedents. It was his grandfather, Yegor Mikhailovich Chekhov, who purchased freedom from serfdom (still in existence when Chekhov was born, though not for long):

> Though he had experienced the horror of slavery in his own person, Yegor Mikhailovich by no means renounced

---

[17] Maxim Litvinov died in 1951 of natural causes, also unusual in the circumstances.

the principle of slavery and oppression for others. Anton Pavlovich remarked that his grandfather had been "a rabid advocate of serfdom."

Naturally, Yermilov did not pause to reflect on the fact that after the Revolution, the highly oppressive regime was replaced by one that was far worse. It is perhaps a general rule that everyone who abominates servitude does not therefore love freedom, especially that of others.

It isn't very long into the book before Yermilov makes what was then and in that place an obligatory reference to Lenin: he, Lenin, would be dragged into any subject whatever. Yermilov writes:

It is one of the ironies of history that precisely from the back-stairs of Russian journalism there emerged a dangerous foe to the Prichibeyevs and Pobedonostsevs, a foe to what Lenin called "the old, accursed, enslaved Russia, the Russia of serfdom and autocracy," an exposer of a way of life so debasing to human beings.[18]

Lenin, of course, was an apostle of the new and even more accursed Russia.

Yermilov begins his summary as follows:

The purifying storm burst and our native land began to

---

[18] Prishibeyev was a fanatic for order in an early story by Chekhov, while Pobedonostsev was the highly reactionary, but also very intelligent, Procurator of the Holy Synod, a kind of non-clerical theocrat.

be turned into a beautiful garden, the laws of its life those of health and beauty.

Commentary is unnecessary, but I wonder what Ivy Litvinov thought of all this as she translated it?

A kind lady from New York sent me a present, a tiny book— or booklet, really—published by the Little Leather Corporation of New York. It was printed, I should imagine, at some time between 1900 and 1914, though it bore no date. It was the kind of present an aspiring but impecunious romantic young man might then have given to a cultivated young lady whom he was trying to impress. It was *Enoch Arden and Other Poems* by Alfred Lord Tennyson. Bound in cheap, thin leather, I doubt the Little Leather Corporation would have given Standard Oil much to worry about in point of capitalisation.

Everyone knows lines from Tennyson, even if he does not know that they are lines from Tennyson (I doubt, for example, that many readers of Agatha Christie remember that the title of one of her books, *The Mirror Crack'd from Side to Side*, is taken from *The Lady of Shalott*). Who now reads Tennyson though, like Byron before him, he made a fortune from his poetry?

I had never read *Enoch Arden* before. It is a narrative poem of many stanzas (and 43 pages in this edition) in which Tennyson achieves something that is not very easy: he writes about three good people for whom one cares equally and who are not boring. It is a sad fact that the goodness of good people seldom makes for exciting reading, as the villainy of even minor villains does.

The story of the poem is that of Enoch Arden, Philip Ray and Annie Lee, childhood friends who live in a fishing village. They play together as children, but 'when the dawn of rosy childhood past', both 'fixt his heart/ On that one girl.' Annie loves Enoch and marries him; Philip accepts with a good grace but loves her still.

Enoch, though poor, is ambitious; he works hard, buys his own boat and prospers. He and Annie are happy; they have three children, one of whom descends into an early grave (not emotional manipulation on Tennyson's part, but more like social realism, given the infant and child mortality of the time).

Enoch, being an estimable man, is offered a job as a boatswain on a trading vessel to China, from which he stands to make a handsome profit. Annie pleads with him not to go, as she fears that if he does so, she will never see him again. He has no such fears, however. He sells his boat to set up Annie in a little shop while he is away, but Annie, having no commercial sense, cannot make a go of it and she and her two surviving children are plunged into poverty. It is to be emphasised that Enoch loves them all dearly and is only doing what he thinks will provide his children with a better childhood than he had as an orphan.

On the return journey from China, Enoch's ship is wrecked and he is marooned on a lush but deserted island, at first with two others but, they dying, soon on his own. There he stays, until rescued ten years later, returning eventually to the village from which he set out so long before.

In the meantime, Philip has wooed Annie and married her,

after a long and virtuous delay. They assume, having had no news of Enoch, that he is dead; and Philip, who in the meantime has prospered and become in effect father to the children, persuades Annie to marry him. They are very happy together and have a further child.

Enoch, unrecognisable, puts up at the village inn run by Miriam Lane, to whom he tells his secret but on her solid oath not to reveal it to Annie or Philip, for to do so would ruin their happiness. Enoch then dies; his tragic sacrifice is that of a good man.

Is this just sentimental guff? I think the Victorians were sometimes more morally flexible than we give them credit for. Once I did some original research on the only murder of a policeman on the island Jersey, which took place in 1846. The victim was George le Cronier and the perpetrator was Madame le Gendre. No more premeditated murder than hers could be imagined; she had the knife with which she stabbed le Cronier specially sharpened for the occasion, which was his forthcoming visit to Mulberry Cottage (still standing) which she ran as a brothel, and which he was determined that she should close. Her mandatory death sentence was commuted to transportation for life to Van Diemen's Land (Tasmania) where she remarried despite the fact that her husband was still alive and in theory still married to her. Although the authorities knew that her marriage in Van Diemen's Land must have been bigamous and therefore criminal, they recognised it without demur.

Before his death, Enoch hides in the garden of Philip's house to catch a glimpse of his beloved wife and children; he does not blame her for what a lesser man might have thought was her infidelity.

> From behind a yew tree there
> That which he better might have shunn'd, if griefs
> Like his have worse or better, Enoch saw...

In other words, there are some situations—not a few, in fact—in which either possible course of action is very unhappy: the essence of tragedy.

In *Lady Clara Vere de Vere*, also in the Little Leather Library corporation's booklet, occurs the famous line, 'Kind hearts are more than coronets.' The following stanza brought back to me a scene that I once witnessed: the poet's subject being an aristocratic lady who is cruel in love for lack of any other interest in her life:

> I know you, Clara Vere de Vere:
>> You pine among your halls and towers:
> The languid light of your proud eyes
>> Is wearied on the rolling hours.
> In glowing health, with boundless wealth,
>> But sickening of a vague disease,
> You know so ill to deal with time,
>> You needs must play such pranks as these.

Once I spent an interesting hour watching very rich women entering and leaving a vastly expensive store in Beverley Hills. It was difficult to say whether they looked more miserable and dissatisfied entering than leaving, in spite of their purchases that should have given them pleasure. They looked more conspicuously bored than do people who perform the most tedious jobs. Probably they felt that dissatisfaction with everything was the highest form of judgment and discrimination.

A lesser-known poem in the booklet is *Sea-Dreams*, whose subject is a man cheated of his meagre savings, the fruit of many years' work by a confidence trickster who makes him buy shares in a non-existent Peruvian goldmine. The poem is 'about', if a poem can be said to be 'about' anything as definite, the need of the wronged person to forgive for his own sake. Tennyson had himself been swindled and the following lines are those of a poet who knows whereof he writes:

> … there was no such mine;
> None; but a gulf of ruin, swallowing gold,
> Not making.

Once again, this called up something in my mind. A friend of mine, a geologist by training, who came to work as a financial promoter, raising money for new mining projects, told me how he used to attend the annual jamboree in Toronto, where such as he gathered to sell their wares, and where promoters met wealthy men with money to invest. There, one year, he was approached by two persons who wanted him to raise money in the City of London on their behalf. They said they had a new goldmine in Venezuela but before agreeing to their request, he insisted on inspecting the site of their alleged mine; but when he got there, being a geologist of experience, he realised at once that the 'mine' was of the Potemkin village variety, erected to dupe the naïve. It was nothing, in fact:

> ... but a gulf of ruin, swallowing gold
> Not making.

He, of course, declined to raise any money on their behalf, but this is not to say that they never found their Tennyson to cheat.

There is a paradox in our attitude to the cuckoo. On the one hand we love to hear the sound of its call, not only because it heralds the arrival of summer, but for its pleasing self. One could not say that the cuckoo's call (entirely male) is a pretty sound, like that of the nightingale's song, but it has a reassuring quality, and everyone loves to hear it, precisely because we know that we shall hear it for only a few weeks a year. (If it were all year round, it would soon be intolerable and drive us to distraction.)

On the other hand, we know the cuckoo to be a wicked bird, parasitising and ruthlessly killing smaller birds, and never picking on anyone its own size. Because of its wickedness, we should rejoice that it is fast disappearing from Britain, but we do not. Cuckoos are in decline in Britain because the birds that they parasitise are in decline, and the latter are in decline because their environment has been destroyed and above all the insects on which they feed have been decimated by pesticides. Even the trees in which the female cuckoos sit to observe the nests in which they will lay their eggs have largely been cut down. Summer may be icumen in, but silent is cuccu.[19]

Because it is so much a larger country, though with the same population, things are not quite as bad in France. While my friend in rural Cambridgeshire has not heard a cuckoo this last ten years or more, we still hear the cuckoo each year in our house in rural France. This year, it competed with the drilling sound of a woodpecker drilling a hollow dead tree[20] and the love-song of the frogs on the riverbank. I suppose that there must be many children who have never heard such sounds, and never will, which is tragic, if it is tragic not to experience nature first-hand. At any rate, without being any kind of naturalist (alas), these sounds of birds and frogs are balm to my soul. When I was a child, there were woodpeckers in London gardens, and starlings and song-thrushes, once common, have almost completely disappeared.

I was completely ignorant of cuckoo biology until I read Nick Davies' wonderful book, *Cuckoo*. Davies, a professor at Cambridge, has studied these birds in the same patch of Cambridgeshire fens for thirty years, happily preserved, testimony to the most disciplined patience and idle curiosity. (My curiosity is always idle.) Until I read his book, I was not even sure whether cuckoos were genetically predetermined to parasitise a particular species of bird, or whether, finding a suitable nest, they adapted their egg, by a mechanism I could not imagine, to resemble that of the species upon which they

---

[19] Summer is icumen in

Lhude sing cuccu...

[20] Later in the year it was the golden orioles who made the most sound.

had chanced. No: cuckoos parasitise the species in whose nest they were raised. They are not adaptable in the way that I thought that they might be. I felt foolish for even having thought of it as a possibility.

Our knowledge of the habits of wild creatures is the result of concentrated intelligence and patience. Professor Davies' hero, as far as the study of cuckoos is concerned, is Edgar Chance, whose book, *The Cuckoo's Secret*, was published in 1922. Chance was a successful businessman (his company made glass syringes, and I remember the name from my childhood because my father dealt with the Chance Company, before the arrival of the disposable plastic syringe that destroyed the market for its syringes), with a passion for ornithology, who collected 25,000 birds' eggs , which would probably now be regarded as a less than praiseworthy thing to do. He gave the collection to the Natural History Museum: there will never be another one like it.

It was Chance who, assisted by others, discovered the cuckoo's method of egg-laying, and he was the first to film it. During the First World War he continued his business (it boomed) and his researches into cuckoos, and like Professor Davies concentrated his observations on a small tract of land. He managed to follow a single cuckoo through four summers, for he discovered that cuckoo's eggs are as individual to them as are fingerprints to us. (I bird nested as a child, mesmerised by the beauty of birds' eggs which I stole from their nests.)

By various manipulations, Chance managed to predict when and where a cuckoo in which he was interested would lay her next egg, and thereby, with cumbersome equipment, filmed her doing so. The bird would swoop down on the nest and lay her egg in a matter of seconds, having spotted the opportunity from a perch high in a tree. Sometimes the parasitised birds—in the case meadow pipits—would seem to welcome the cuckoo's attention, as if flattered by it, but sometimes would attack the cuckoo and try to drive it away. This variation in response is itself remarkable, and once Chance observed a pipit, very much smaller than a cuckoo, with a bill of cuckoo feathers which it had aggressively plucked from a cuckoo while attacking it.

I know that evolutionary theory can explain the evolution of the cuckoo's life cycle, because it can explain everything. But I confess that I find it difficult to be convinced by any evolutionary theory of the cuckoo's conduct, though the fault is mine. Did the cuckoo develop its migratory habits bit by bit or all at once, extending the migration by a few miles, or a few hundred miles, every generation?

Chance begins his book, which contains some rather blurred photos of cuckoos flying away from nests, with one of the host's eggs in its bill which it has replaced with an egg of its own. The system is efficient, because the cuckoo eats the egg it steals. Chance says:

> Probably no bird has taken a more conspicuous place in the interests of mankind than the common Cuckoo.

Chance so loves his birds that he always capitalises their name.

On seeing his silent film of the behaviour of cuckoos, one spectator wrote to him eloquently:

Perhaps the scene which impressed me most was that of the ejection of the young Pipits by the newly-hatched Cuckoo. It was a glimpse into the appalling cruelties of the struggle for existence, the 'survival of the fittest' whose motto is 'Might is right.' It offended, so to speak, every rule of fair play that appeals to one's sporting instinct. The young interloper was obviously very much better equipped for the struggle, blind as he and nest-fellows were, with his long unfledged flippers... Most horrible of all, however, was the cold- blooded unconcern of the mother Pipit, whose attitude might have been expressed by her saying, 'Hurry up and get the job over, so that we can have a moment's peace.'

My copy of Chance's book once belonged to H.P. Fairlie, and he bought it in May 1922. The miracle of the internet allowed me to discover that H.P. Fairlie was almost certainly Henry Prescott Fairlie, co-author of *Handbook of Anaesthetics* that went through more than one edition, and who was almost certainly an amateur ornithologist. In 1912, he wrote a thesis titled *A Comparison of the Relative Value of Chloroform and Ether in General Anaesthesia with Special Reference to Their Influence on the Blood Pressure*. The thesis is available online:

Case III: A muscular man who drank heavily. Probably owing to the presence of chronic bronchitis, chloroform caused coughing.

In 1916, Dr Fairlie applied to join the Royal Army Medical Corps for service in the First World War:

I am prepared to render the service or services marked above (general medical service).

In support of his application, he wrote:

I am at present giving anaesthetics and for the past year, at Springburn Red Cross Hospital. If my services as an anaesthetist are urgently required and if a reasonable financial position is guaranteed in view of the above responsibilities, I am quite willing to offer my services.

This suggests less than patriotic fervour on his part. Whether his proposition was successful, I do not know (I also did not know that you could bargain with the army like that, or that anyone would even attempt to do so). At any rate, Dr Fairlie survived the First World War to buy *The Cuckoo's Secret*.

The internet is a marvel. Without it, how would I have ever learnt of the existence of Henry Prescott Fairlie, or anything about him? It would have been the work of a lifetime—never undertaken, of course—instead of that of a few seconds.

When I was about fourteen, I played the part of Crichton in J.M. Barrie's play, *The Admirable Crichton*. Among my many inabilities is an inability to act, though being somewhat obsequious or pusillanimous by nature (except in print) I managed well enough while Crichton, the butler who turned leader when he and the family he served were stranded on a desert island, remained in the character of butler. I managed much less well when he became leader, however. I found it easy to act humble, even if, deep inside, I have never been humble. I found it difficult to act as if I were forceful.

It was in the pleasant little town of Beaumaris, on the Menai Strait on the Anglesey side, that I happened across a little book by Jerome K. Jerome in a junk shop or emporium of antiques. It was the text of a play, *Fanny and the Servant Problem*, published in 1909, the year of my father's birth. I am unsure whether it was ever performed, for the book did not have a cast of the first performance, as such first editions of plays usually do, and the instruction to amateur groups that wanted to stage the play were enjoined to contact the theatrical agents and publishers, Samuel French Ltd., for permission to do so, perhaps more in hope than expectation.

At any rate, the play had quite a lot in common with *The Admirable Crichton*, written seven years before. Its main character is Fanny, a music hall artiste with whom Vernon Wetherell, Lord Bantock, has fallen in love and married in Paris without having revealed to her that he is a peer of the realm. He wanted her to marry him for himself, not for his title or his lands. At the same time, she disguised from him that her family were all in service, a family from which she ran away to join the circus, so to speak. At the instigation of her theatrical manager, she tells Lord Bantock that she has as relatives a bishop in New Zealand and a judge in Ohio, to make it appear that her family is one of distinction. While Lord Bantock has not revealed his true identity as a peer, it is clear that he was of the upper echelons of society.

Fanny arrives at Bantock Hall still unaware of the status of her husband. His maiden aunts and twenty-three servants, the latter of whom are Fanny's relatives, had been horrified by the news that Vernon has married so far beneath him, an actress and therefore by definition a low-class adventuress. The servants are as snobbish as the maiden aunts; they have made the aristocratic scale of values their own and are, if anything, more rigid in their class distinctions than the aristocrats themselves. When the butler, the head both of the servants and Fanny's family, the Bennets, realises that his niece, Fanny, is the new Lady Bantock, he is determined to take her in hand and teach her how she ought to behave. The Bennet family, moreover, is narrowly and sanctimoniously religious in low church fashion and holds prayer meetings somewhere in the subterranean depths of the house and are now all the more fervent because they have a sinner, Fanny, in their midst.

The new Lady Bantock's former manager, George P. Newte, a man cheerfully vulgar but of good heart, pays a visit to Bantock Hall while Lord Bantock is out hunting. The butler, Bennet, refuses at first to admit him upstairs, since he is not a gentleman, hoping to give him a glass of beer and sending him on his way. Lady Bantock insists, however, on his admission to the drawing room, and gradually she bends the scandalised servants to her will. Finally, the servants—her relatives—accept that she is the new Lady Bantock and not merely the rebellious girl who ran away to work in a music hall.

The play mostly takes place in Lady Bantock's room or boudoir, in which there is a portrait of the first Lady Bantock by Hoppner. The latter was a painter more highly regarded when Jerome K. Jerome wrote the play than he is now, his paintings fetching astronomical prices at the time. What would then have cost the equivalent of £1,000,000 would now cost perhaps £5,000, so far has he fallen out of fashion. But the playgoers of the time, if there ever were any, would have understood the significance of a Hoppner on the wall as a sign of social prominence and great wealth.

Towards the end of the play, it is revealed that the first Lady Bantock, who was an exceptional beauty, was in fact the daughter of a butcher, despite her aristocratic mien.

The play could be taken either as a satire on the British class system or a paean of praise to it: for it is a fact that much of the British aristocracy is not of ancient lineage, and two, three or four generations back there lurks an ironmaster or someone engaged in ignoble but lucrative trade. Male aristocrats often married beneath themselves, if the women were particularly beautiful or fascinating. Jerome K. Jerome's play could be taken as a puncturing of aristocratic pretension and mores, as something that could be learned, as dentistry can be learned.

That is no doubt how most people would take it, but other lessons could be drawn from it. True enough, the aristocratic lifestyle was not necessarily inherited in a quasi-genetic or even congenital fashion; it was something that could be attained and imitated. It was a lodestar which the ambitious could follow, and insofar as the aristocracy generally had refined tastes, even if not highly intellectual, it acted as a refiner of manners and aesthetics. The upper bourgeoisie aspired to aristocratic style, as the lower orders did to bourgeois: thus the aristocracy, without necessarily intending to, exerted an elevating effect on the whole population. The system was unfair and unjust, perhaps, but not without its redeeming features. One has only to see the terrible and hideous mansions that modern billionaires build themselves to see what the absence of an aristocratic element has on taste and the arts. And one has only to see a photograph of Jerome K. Jerome, born into the lower middle class and raised on the verge of poverty, to see what an effect of aristocratic style had upon him: no billionaire chief-executive T-shirts for him!

We often forget that a class society is not necessarily a closed society, and that social climbing is probably no worse a vice than is the aping of the poor by people who are rich (and who are usually intent upon becoming even richer).

The only work by Jerome K. Jerome that I had read before this play was *Three Men in a Boat*, by which I suspect he is now exclusively remembered. But I also associate him in my mind with something else. A formerly Russian friend of mine, who had studied at Moscow's Foreign Languages Institute, learnt English so perfectly that you would think it was his mother tongue. He became a British citizen but once made a tiny mistake that we said proved that he had been a KGB spy all along. I cannot remember the context, but I once mentioned *Three Men in a Boat* in his presence.

'By Jerome Jerome,' he said.

'Aha!' I exclaimed, as did my wife, who is French. 'So, you are a KGB spy after all!'

No English person would have called Jerome K. Jerome *Jerome Jerome*. Men have been shot for less, and my friend, who could hardly have been more anti-Soviet, was mortified by this miniscule but revelatory error.

It was seven years since I had last been to the pleasant town of Lewes in Sussex. I was speaking at the same literary festival as the last time I visited, having just published a book. That time, I was the penultimate speaker of the whole festival, but the last speaker was a controversial journalist by the name of Katie Hopkins. She was prevented from speaking by a mob calling themselves anti-fascist, though they looked and behaved exactly as fascists would themselves have behaved. The festival was held in a deconsecrated church which the fascist anti-fascists besieged, and we had to be led out under cover of darkness through the neglected and overgrown churchyard at the rear, escorted by the police. Some people were truly frightened, and I suspect that had the mob been able to lay its hands on Katie Hopkins, it might have done her some damage, if not torn her limb from limb—for the good of humanity, of course.

On my second occasion, alas, I had little time to visit the three second-hand bookshops on the High Street: a highly unusual concentration of such shops. On the last occasion, I had more leisure to browse them and even thought of writing an entire book based upon the books I bought in them, for example a first edition of Walter Scott's *Heart of Midlothian*. This time, however, I had very little time to browse. Only one of the bookshops opened on Sunday, the *Fifteenth Century Bookshop*, so-called because of the building in which it is located, and I had an hour in it after I gave my talk and before it closed. On the following Monday, I had a quarter of an hour in the *Bow Window Bookshop* which opened at 10 am, before I caught my 10.25 train to London. I could happily have spent ten times as long there, but I bought three books quickly, to the pleased astonishment of the bookseller, who was presumably more used to dithering customers.

'You are a very efficient browser,' he said to me, the highest—possibly the only—compliment a bookseller has ever paid me.

One of the books that I bought was the first American edition of Vita Sackville-West's novel, or novella, *Seducers in Ecuador*. It was just the right size, volume and length for a train journey. No doubt it was a sign of my literary under-education that I had not heard of it before. I was seduced by its title and its first sentence: 'It was in Egypt that Arthur Lomax contracted the habit which, after a pleasantly varied career, brought him finally to the scaffold.' Another extraneous reason for choosing it was that it was first published (in its English edition) in 1924, precisely a hundred years ago as I write this. Why such anniversaries exercise a hold on us is an interesting question to which I have not seen the answer.

I cannot say that I otherwise started with a strong predilection in its favour. This was because it was dedicated to Virginia Woolf, a figure for whom I have limited esteem, not least because of the exaggerated esteem in which she is held by others; but I must say in all fairness that the novella was, especially at its beginning, not only captivating but very well-written. Virginia Woolf somewhat decried her friend's and future lover's ease of writing, facility in her view being the origin of the facile. (A second cousin of mine, of literary inclination, who had once lived in Bohemian Paris and had been for a while the lover of Richard Wright, author of *Native Son*, accused me of the same fault.)

The story of *Seducers in Ecuador* is easily told. Arthur Lomax, of the first sentence, is recruited by Bellamy, a fellow-member of his club, to join him on his yacht sailing to Egypt. Bellamy is, of course, a very rich man, but bored. Also on board, recruited almost at random, are Miss Whitaker, a woman of indeterminate background, who spends much of her time writing letters to a supposed lover in Ecuador, and Artival, a biologist.

Lomax is in love with a married woman, Marian Vane, who requites his love, but she is married so that a true liaison is impossible for her (this is 1924, not 2024). Impulsively, Lomax and Miss Whitaker leave the yacht in Cairo and secretly marry. Bellamy reveals to Lomax that he has a fatal disease and asks the latter, as an act of friendship, to administer drugs that will kill him. This Lomax does once they return to England, Bellamy, unbeknownst to him, having left him his immense fortune. Sentenced to hang for murder, the post-mortem having revealed that Bellamy had nothing wrong with him, Lomax leaves the fortune to Artival, whom he hardly knows. The last paragraph is as follows:

> Shortly after Lomax had been hanged, Bellamy's nearest relations, three maiden ladies who lived in Hampstead and interested themselves in the conversion of the heathen, entered a plea that Bellamy's will had been composed under the undue influence of Arthur Lomax. The case was easily proved, and it was understood that the bulk of the fortune would be placed by the next-of-kin as conscience money at the disposal of His Majesty's Treasury.

I fear to be considered too literal-minded, but surely Lomax would not be deemed to have inherited Bellamy's estate if found guilty of having murdered him? But absence of verisimilitude is not, perhaps, a very strong literary criticism, unless art should always imitate life.

In Egypt, says the author, most tourists wear blue spectacles, the sunglasses of their time, and Arthur Lomax 'followed this prudent if unbecoming fashion.' He was, in fact, a Bloomsbury type:

> Lomax was less interested in the Sphinx than in the phenomenon produced by wearing these coloured glasses. In fact, he had already dismissed the Sphinx as a most over-rated object. But, as so often happens, although disappointed in one quarter, he had been richly and unexpectedly rewarded in another. The world was changed for him, and, had he but known it, the whole of his future altered, by those two circles of blue glass.

One might say that the act of perception became more interesting to him than anything perceived, an attitude that was to become fateful, at least in literary circles:

> Whether he pushed the glasses up on to his forehead, and looked out from underneath them, or slid them down on the tip of his nose, and looked out above them, he confronted unaided the too realistic glare of the Egyptian sun. When, however, he readjusted them to the place where they were intended to be worn, he immediately resented the curious world so recently become his own.

It was more than curious; it was magical... he resolved, however, not to initiate a soul into his discovery. To those blessed with perception, let perception remain sacred, but let the obtuse dwell for ever in their darkness.

This is well-written, but I could not help but wonder whether it expressed, not perhaps fully consciously, the fundamental, and fundamentally snobbish, philosophy of the Bloomsbury group: that there were those whose perceptions were superior and sacred, and those who perceived hardly anything at all, the elect and the rest.

As I have mentioned, the Fifteenth Century Bookshop is so called because it is in a fifteenth century building, not because it sells fifteenth century books.

Not all second-hand bookshops are created equal, and the stock of this bookshop is not nearly as refined or bibliophilic as that of the Bow Window Bookshop—and is much cheaper. It is the kind of bookshop in which the works of popular writers of the past eight or nine decades, no longer much read, are to be found in profusion, the clientele not worrying too much about the edition or even the condition of the books. They buy for content, not appearance, much less for investment or speculation, though what content there is in once best-selling authors such as Warwick Deeping or Dornford Yates I have yet to discover.

I selected three titles and took them a little shamefacedly to the owner of the bookshop, unusually a woman (book obsession is overwhelmingly a male affliction). I told her that my wife would not be at all pleased with my purchases, but she said that you can never have enough books, as the Duchess of Windsor once said that you can never have enough money. It was clear that she did not mean by this that the purchase of books was good for her business, but that it was good for the soul—even if they rested on the shelves.

The first of the books I bought was *The Dancing Coachman and other Verses* by J.B. Morton. For some reason, I misread the author's name as H.V. Morton, perhaps because the latter's travel books are always to be found in such bookshops, mouldering as fodder for the silverfish. No one reads him now, though he sold by the hundreds of thousands in the 1920s and 30s, both in Britain and America. In fact, as I subsequently discovered, J.B. Morton, though no relative, worked on the *Daily Express* at the same time as H.V. and shared some of his prejudices.

By deceiving Chance, I opened *The Dancing Coachman* at page 34, on which there was the mildly satirical verse, *Playing the Game*. It was the best verse in the book and thinking that the others would be of the same quality, I bought the book. In the 1920s and 30s, many writers tried their hand at comic verse, for which there was a vogue though the genre is not much esteemed today. Apart from anything else, it demands scansion and rhyme, and thus imposes both a discipline and limitations, as does the genre of the crime novel.

The poem begins:

> I hope I shall avoid offence
> In praising English common sense...

and continues:

> While having no desire to shock
> The people of inferior stock—
> By which I mean queer[21] Frenchman who
> Brandish their arms, and shout at you,
> Italians with mandolins,
> And Spaniards with unshaven chins;
> All those who, by freak of fate,
> Born in some tinpot Latin State,
> Are doomed to live un-English lives,
> And even marry foreign wives…

It continues in this amusing and ironical fashion, and concludes:

> Straight is our bat, our cricket clean,
> And, above all—Don't Make a Scene.

I have to admit that the avoidance of scenes is one of the aims of my life, and on my tombstone, if I am not incinerated, I hope will be inscribed the words, 'He made no fuss.'

In view of the author's geniality and ironical view of the English, it was a little surprising to find, on page 72, the following, slightly unpleasant lines that would probably not be published today:

> I know a pair of yellow Jews

---

[21] A word then still meaning strange rather than homosexual.

Who make a mint of money
By selling leaky boot and shoes—
They thought it frightfully funny.
The shoes were twice the normal price,
But labour was requited,
For one fine day, I'm proud to say,
The dirty beasts were knighted.

In two other little poems, the author returned to the fray, as it were:

When Schmell and Schwein go ratting
You can tell them from the rats
By the way the ferrets cut them[22],
And because they both wear hats.

The poem is called *City Men at Play*: they are therefore financiers and hence metaphorical rats themselves. And in another poem called *Epitaph for a War Profiteer*, we read:

Here lies the profiteer Kastenfelstein,
Called latterly Fitzwarren,
There is some corner of an English field
That is forever foreign.

This is undeniably clever. There is an obvious reference to Rupert Brooke's famous lines:

---

[22] Deliberately ignore them socially.

> If I should die think only this of me,
> That there's some corner of a foreign field
> That is forever England.

It is a reference, too, to the fact that many people of German surname changed to a more English name during the First World War (including the Royal Family, of course) to avoid xenophobic opprobrium and even violence. The eminent physician, Arthur Hertz, a cousin of the great physicist, Heinrich Hertz, published his lengthy volume on the problem of constipation under his own name in 1909, but changed it to Arthur Hurst during the war, was knighted, and published his *magnum opus*, *Diseases of War*, under the name of Sir Arthur Hirst. Who could really blame him for not wishing to be the object of ignorant mob violence? But J.B. Morton would have seen in this something sinister and underhand.[23]

J.B. Morton's life coincided almost exactly with that of A.P. Herbert's, who also wrote light, amusing, mildly satirical verse. Both had served in the First World War, and both wrote serious novels about their experiences before turning to humour as a genre. Morton wrote a weekly column in the *Daily Express* for more than fifty years afterwards, and Herbert was similarly prolific.

As I mentioned, I mistook J.B. for H.V. (perhaps this goes

---

[23] Sir Arthur Hurst's son, Christopher, founded the splendid, and even noble, independent publisher, C. Hurst and Company.

to prove Karl Popper's view that there is no perception that is free of theoretical presupposition). They were not related but worked at the same time on the same newspaper. H.V. Morton's most famous travel book, *In Search of England*, sold more than half a million copies, from which I deduced, without having read it, that it must have been of low quality. But I was curious about Morton, of whom I knew nothing, and bought an excellent biography of him by Michael Bartholomew, of whom I also knew nothing.

Bartholomew discovered, by reading Morton's unpublished diaries, that this Morton, too, was an antisemite, indeed a much more virulent one than his namesake. He was in private a Nazi sympathiser, though he commanded, apparently with devotion, a brigade of the Home Guard during the war. He never expressed his prejudices or his sympathies in public, either before or during the war, in order to preserve his image as a genial, tolerant person.

In fact, he was a talented writer and very far from stupid. His biographer does not much care for him as a man, but he recognises his ability. He calls his biography *In Search of H.V. Morton* because Morton's most famous books were titled *In Search of...* somewhere or other. No other book about him exists, or probably ever will. He was a very private man, perhaps because he was so sexually predatory. Batholomew quotes a sentence from Morton's book *In Search of Ireland* describing a visit to the Guinness brewery:

Yeast is added to assist fermentation, and as you look through a door you see this khaki-coloured scum moving in a slow, repulsive manner, opening and closing a bubbly eye here and there with a kind of obscene intelligence.

This is surely brilliant writing, and no one can write such a sentence by accident.

According to a friend of mine, a celebrity is someone of whom he has never heard. I am rather the same: I could bump into someone world-famous and ask him, quite genuinely, what he did for a living. As I am sometimes supposed to be a social commentator and cultural critic, this is perhaps not to my credit. But as another of my friends put it with regard to rap music, you don't have to taste the whole pound of butter to know that it's rancid.

The British journalist, Lynn Barber, was once famous for her interviews with celebrities, of most of whom (not quite all) I had not heard of, and of whom I knew nothing. Three years older than I, she was much more interested in youth culture than I ever was and seems not to have grown out of her infatuation with it. I became interested in her myself when I read a short book by her, published in the year I write this, titled *A Little Art Education*. It consists of accounts of her meetings with contemporary artists, the work of a good proportion of whom seems to me utterly worthless except in the financial sense (and that only, I suspect, for a short period, until the bubble of the art equivalent of the Tulipomania bursts). The author seems to me to be lacking in discrimination, failing to distinguish between a real artist,

Howard Hodgkin, and some of her subjects who seem to me to indulge in what might be called *para-artistic* activity: that is to say, they go through all the agonies of creation, live unconventional lives, exhibit what they create, but whose work is the thinnest of thin gruel to the mind, soul, or aesthetic sense. But the author is dazzled by the way they live and talk, as if those were the most important attributes of artists.

I never read her interviews with celebrities when they appeared in *The Observer*, because I was not interested in the people whom she interviewed, though she had a reputation for extracting sensational revelations from them. I find the very word *celebrity* off-putting, and I am more interested in the lives of ratcatchers or insurance-loss adjustors. The latter are particularly fascinating, and give you a wonderful insight into human nature, or at least into an aspect of it. Ratcatchers, too, are interesting, especially on the subject or rats, for which (or is it for whom?) they have a great respect. They are extremely knowledgeable. In the days when there was a municipal ratcatcher, we called him because there was a terrible, half-sweet smell emanating from below our dining-room. In short, we smelt a rat. The ratcatcher told us that we had two choices: he could take up the floorboards for him to find and remove it, or we could leave it where it was, in which case the smell would go in exactly six weeks. And in exactly six weeks, the smell did go, just as he said it would, which gave us great respect for the ratcatcher, who struck us in any case as a good deal more competent than most municipal officials, possibly because he loved his work. Naturally, when redundancies came, he was the first to go. Rat-catching was for him a vocation, not just a job, and the last thing a bureaucracy needs or wants these days is a man with a vocation. He sets such a bad example.

Anyway, I decided to procure and read Lynn Barber's memoir of interviews with celebrities, *A Curious Career*. The very brilliant people I have known have not been interested in acquiring celebrity, and none of them has actually acquired it, at least not in the sense of being recognisable to multitudes in the street or of feeling annoyed when they fail to be thus recognised. I have never met anyone with a publicity agent, for example, and the brilliance of the brilliant people I have known has been in their work, not their self-promotion. None behaved in the petulant, spoilt-child manner of some of Lynn Barber's interviewees.

Barber became known for her ability, like that of a police questioner, to get her subjects to self-incriminate, such that it was remarkable in the end that anyone would agree to be interviewed by her. They were the kind of people, I suppose, who are increasing in number, for whom any public exposure is better than none. She was sometimes called the Demon Barber, that is to say Sweeney Todd, the Fleet Street barber who turned his customers into sausages. She was not confrontational or strident; she preferred her subjects, or victims, to impale themselves. Open-ended questions invited answers that were more revealing than specific and hostile questions would ever have done.

But her interviews were with people whose celebrity, I suspect, and perhaps hope, will not last long. Celebrity is one of those qualities that deliquesces. Here she goes to Dublin to interview a man called Shane McGowan, a singer:

I was prepared for the teeth, the famous blackened stumps, but the suit is an unanticipated horror show, with its thickening patina of stains down the trousers culminating in big blobby splatters on the shoes. If he had not been sick down his trousers several dozen times, he must have a very good stylist. His skin has the shiny pallor of someone who has never seen the daylight.

I hope I shall not be thought prissily fastidious when I say that I do not find this attractive. I suppose that if I were interviewing Mozart or Newton I might think it worthwhile to overlook so vile an appearance, but surely not in the case of a member of a group called *The Pogues*. Nor did he say anything particularly interesting because he was already too far gone on gin and tonic. Barber says:

> Later in the evening, Shane and Gerry [former owner of Filthy MacNasty's bar in Islington] announce that they have decided that they can trust me, so they will cut me in on the bank robbery they are doing tomorrow. They are driving to a country town, about an hour out of Dublin, and they need a getaway driver. 'She'd be a fucking brilliant getaway driver,' Shane opines.

A little later, she writes with the kind of false sophistication of those who value sophistication or the avoidance of the obvious for its own sake:

> What did I feel about robbing a bank—I don't mind robbing a bank per se but presumably the money was

meant to go to the IRA and did I actually want to support the IRA? Would I mind being caught—I felt we were bound to be—and going to prison? And if I did go to prison, what would happen to my cats? Ah—salvation. My cats seem to have acted as my lifeline to sanity during this period. I couldn't rob a bank with Shane MacGowan because then I would go to prison and my cats would be put down. Problem solved. Nevertheless I played the Pogues obsessively for months and felt a lingering guilt that I broke my promise to rob a bank with Shane MacGowan.

Lynn Barber was fifty-six when she wrote this adolescent, facetious tripe for *The Observer*, Britain's most serious, or solemn, Sunday newspaper, and deemed it worthy of reprint when she was sixty-nine.

I no longer recollect how I came by my five volumes of the *Harleian Miscellany*, edited by Doctor Johnson and printed by Thomas Osborne in the 1740s. They are, alas, not in the best of condition, though booksellers would no doubt praise the condition of the actual pages, which are unmarked. The title page reads:

The Harleian Miscellany or, a Collection of Scarce, Curious,
And Entertaining Pamphlets and Tracts, As Well in Manuscript as in print,

Found in the late Earl of Oxford's Library

There are strange coincidences in this life (as, indeed, it would be strange of there were not, considering of how many billions of events a life consists), one of these being that I opened the second of the volumes to a tract titled '*The Honour of* Gout: or a rational Discourse, demonstrating that the *Gout* is one of the *greatest Blessings* which can befall mortal Man; that all Gentlemen, who are *weary* of it, are their own Enemies; that those *Practitioners*, who offer at the *Cure*, at the verist and most mischievous *Cheats* in Nature.' It was 'by Way of a Letter to an eminent Citizen, wrote in the Heat of a violent Paroxysm, and now published for the Common Good.' It was dated 1699.

The coincidence was that I was suffering myself from gout at the time as I leafed through the hefty volume. I am, according to the author, one of those most fortunate beings who inherited gout, not having had to overindulge in wine or women in order to contract it and benefit from its many advantages.

I remember the very day when my father had his first attack. It came to him like a rifle shot from a sniper, with exactly that suddenness. Almost immediately, his joint in his right big toe swelled and reddened. The pain was so acute and the joint so tender that not only could he not bear the weight of a sheet upon his foot but could not bear for someone to enter the room in which he was lying, in case he should disturb the air and set off the pain again. My own few episodes have been much less severe, though the first was mildly inconvenient. I was giving a public lecture in Berlin and had to remove my shoe, thereafter hobbling round the lecture hall on one unstockinged foot. The Germans in the audience probably thought that this was normal British behaviour.

But what, according to this tract, are the advantages of gout to the sufferer? Even in my youth, when it was less prevalent than it is now, it had the reputation of afflicting those of high social status and superior intelligence, and of protecting them from coronary artery disease. There was a certain cachet attached to suffering from it.

The author of the tract, who combines facetiousness and irony with seriousness, such that it is not always possible to distinguish one from the other, lists the great benefits of gout under six heads.

The first is that 'the Gout gives a man Pain without Danger.' The author admits that the sufferer might be reluctant to acknowledge this, for 'Sickness and Peevishness commonly go together.' But at other times he will admit that pain without danger is a blessed thing. When men are ill, they fear death and did any man, the author asks, ever die of the Gout? When a man is ill, he fears only to die, and once he knows that he has the Gout, he knows that he will survive. When a man has the Gout, he is so safe from death that even doctors cannot kill him.

Second, 'the Gout is no constant Companion, but allows his patients lucid joyous intervals.' The author says that 'Human Nature is so framed that no one Thing is agreeable to it always; therefore it is as well for us, that the World is so full of Changes. Therefore, also, the Gout by coming and going, provides not only variety which is necessary, but how often have I heard a grave Advice, one that had tried Health and Sickness, alternately, for many Years, tell the robust young, riotous Fellow, that he knew not the value of Health.' Indeed, 'how should he, having never been sick?' How should he understand 'the Deliciousness of it'? If he gets the Gout, 'he will thoroughly understand the matter.' In other words, the Gout is like whipping: it's nice when it stops, and you can never know that you are well until you have been ill.

Third, 'The Gout presents you with a perpetual Almanack', by which the author means a weather forecast. 'People of the best sense,' says the author, 'are proud to publish the Satisfaction they take... which the Gout affords them... for instance, as to the Foreknowledge of the Weather.'

Fourth, 'Gouty Persons are most free from the Headache,' which is because the impurities of the blood which cause both descend in Gout to the feet, thus sparing the head. This, says the author, explains why amputees are so sexually potent: the nutritive properties of the blood are freed of their dilution caused by feeding the limbs, and therefore feed the genitalia the more.

Fifth, 'the Gout preserves its patients from the Great Danger of Fevers.' The Gout, he continues, acts like Purgatory, 'which sets them [the people in it] out of the Danger of the Lake [the fiery lake of Hell], and renders them (like burnt Tobacco-pipes) clean and pure, and fit for Paradise.' This, he said, is the true picture of the effects of the Gout; and if people object on theological grounds that Purgatory does not exist, the reader is to remember 'That a false Story may be a true Picture, and serve to illustrate as necessary a Doctrine as that of Purgatory.' Be that as it may, the author illustrates the undoubted fact—undoubted by him—'the purging Fires of the Gout withdraw the Fewel [fuel] from the destructive Fires of burning Fevers.'

Sixth:

> To crown the Honour of the Gout, it is not to be cured.
> The Gout defies all your gross Galenical Methods, and
> all your Exalted Chymical Preparations; for the conjunct
> causes thereof… lie in Parts so very remote, that the
> Virtues of no Medicines can reach them; and, Heaven be
> praised for it, for why, Sir, would you cure (as you call it)
> the Gout, which gives you Pain without Danger, the
> better Taste of Health, by an Acquaintance with Pain, a
> Knowledge of Future Things, Freedom from the Head-
> ach, and from Fevers… I you and I, Sir… shall neither
> of us ever tamper with the Doctor for the Cure of the
> Gout, which rally and truly is incurable, unless the
> patient be killed; which is what the Doctor of medicine
> aims at, perhaps not what he directly aims at himself. For
> his Heart is chiefly upon his Fee; his Prayers that his
> Patient may neither die nor recover, at least not die, while
> he is worth a Penny; but when his last Penny is spent,
> then the miserable creature is forsaken…

There is but one drawback to the Gout, of which it is said,
'Drink Claret, and have the Gout, and drink no Claret and
still have the Gout.' It, the Gout, therefore acts as no deterrent
to those who whose intemperance or lustfulness brings it on,
for 'gouty once, gouty for ever.'

For the moment, however, my gout is in abeyance.

I have often wondered what I would have done at the outbreak of the First World War, had I been of military age. I don't think I should have had the courage to be a conscientious objector, or the clear-sightedness either. But neither would my decision to join up have been pure moral cowardice: it would have partaken of guilt and shame at seeing others go off to war and holding myself aloof. I think that consideration of whether the cause was good or bad would not have weighed very greatly in my mind.

I have already mentioned that the first book of the humourist J.B. Morton was a serious novel published in 1919 about the Great War. As far as I know, he never wrote anything serious again, and it is difficult to believe that the decision not to do so was anything but a conscious decision to put the war behind him, for (to judge from the book) he saw such things that could be put to the back of a mind only by deliberate policy to do so. What, after all, would have been the point of dwelling on them (an unfashionable question)?

The book's title is *The Barber of Putney* and is the story of Tim Hinrick, a petty bourgeois who runs a barber's shop in Putney. There is only one class that the intelligentsia hates more than the bourgeois, and that is the petty bourgeois, about whom never a good word is said, especially as Adolf Hitler came from it, but J.B. Morton does not share this prejudice. Tim Hinrick is a hero of the quiet type.

I would not claim that *The Barber of Putney* is one of the great war books, but it nevertheless has memorable scenes. Nor is it straightforwardly an anti-war novel, though it in no way covers up or disguises the horrors of war. It is not uncommon for people who have gone through terrible horrors to find something of value, in the context of their own lives, in what they have gone through—and survived, of course. The value lessens the pain.

When I was a young doctor, I met Dr Jay Nardini, an American doctor who had been captured by the Japanese in the Philippines at the outset of the war. By the time of his liberation, half of his unit had starved to death; he himself weighed less than eighty pounds and he suffered from beriberi (about which he wrote a paper after the war). After I had made the normal clucking noises about how terrible it must have been, he said something that has stayed with me. Viewed many years later, he said, he was glad to have experienced what he did, for all else that he experienced afterwards could not rise above the level of mere inconvenience.

There are a few fine scenes in Morton's book, for example when the newly-married Tim takes his departure for the war. Both he and his bride know clearly that he might be killed (even though he does not yet know the scale of the horrors he is about to endure). They are almost shy as they say goodbye to one another, but the emotion is all the deeper for not being openly expressed. If Morton is accurate (and I think he is), ordinary people in those days understood that the implicit was deeper and more powerful than the explicit: and this understanding came not from formal education, for Tim Hinrick is not a highly educated man in the formal sense, but from the general culture and understanding of life of the population. Before he departs for the front:

> They walked a long way... there must have been long

silences, for they were silent when they came back...
They found a tea-shop and sat opposite to each other,
not troubling to notice the people round them, and both
made a show of eating cakes. They laughed at the most
absurd remarks and the most trivial incidents. Somebody
dropped a bun. That was something to talk about.

Back home, Tim kept looking at the clock. 'Well —' he
said, and paused. 'Time?' 'Think so.' 'Got everything?'
'Yes, dear,' Well, good-bye, Tim. Shall I come to the
station?' 'I wouldn't, Meg. Crush and all that, you know,'
and—'Right, Mind you write whenever you can.'

Who could doubt that this conveys deeper emotion than
more demonstrative words ever would?

Allied to this is the sense of humour shown by people who
had very little reason to laugh. A commonsensical non-
commissioned officer tells Tim that at the front, 'If you lose
your 'ead, you'll lose your 'ead.' When a man is shot through
the jaw, someone says, ''E's been to the dentist.' (This is the
opposite of callous, as modern sensibility would have it.) When
a soldier who has been in action turns up in Tim's camp and
Tim asks him where he's been, he replies, 'Collecting
butterflies, of course.'

But there is no attempt to edulcorate the horrors of war:

Often they had to tread on bodies and once Tim slipped,
and his hand came in contact with soft, cold pulp. In
another place he saw a boot and a leg up to the knee,
with the puttee on it, sticking out of the earth. He saw
worse things than that. He saw things that cannot be

written down even in a book of war.

One of Tim's closest friends in the army, a man of higher social class than Tim, and a poet who has refused to apply for a commission because he wants to stay close to the salt of the earth, is killed, and his regimental officer writes to his fiancée, telling her how proud of him is his regiment and how 'he will be missed more than I can say.' Tim also writes to her: 'We knew what he was like and we look up to him as everybody must who knew him.'

After my mother died in 2006, I found in her papers a telegram from the War Office informing her of how her fiancé, an RAF fighter pilot in the defence of Malta, was reported missing and must be presumed dead. An officer wrote to say that he was a very gallant gentleman. A fellow airman wrote to describe how he had died and that he had been very brave and would be missed more than he could say. Among the letters was the one that he wrote to my mother on the very eve of his death.

I often wonder what I should have been like if he had been my father: an absurd question, of course, because had he been my father, I should not have been I. Despite its absurdity, though, I cannot help asking myself the question.

My copy of Morton's book, in a Penguin edition, was printed in November 1939, two months or so into the war. Included in it is the preface that Morton wrote to another edition six years before and which explains why a book containing vivid descriptions of the horrors of war would not have been considered inimical to the war effort in 1939. Morton makes clear that his book was not of standard anti-war issue:

> The barber in my book went out to fight because it was his duty, and because he was too sane to sneer at the word 'hazard.' But if we are to discuss emotion, I prefer anyhow the emotion which led young men to leave homes and families, endure the extremes of discomfort and danger, and finally to lay down their lives—I infinitely prefer such an emotion to the miserable mass-hysteria of pacifism, which teaches every man to regard himself as the centre of his world, and this life as his most precious possession.

As exam papers used to say when calling for an essay on a contentious proposition, 'Discuss'.

As I have mentioned, in the aftermath of the First World War, there was a vogue in England for comic verse, often by men who had been through it and were wounded in it. Laughter was, perhaps, the only thing that could keep despair at bay.

One of the comic poets was E.V. Knox (1881-1971), who was for many years the editor of the now defunct English humorous magazine, *Punch*, and had fought and been injured in the war. In 1926, he published a little book of comic verse, one of many, titled *Poems of Impudence*.

> The tiniest pebble on the beach
> A lesson to us all can teach.

The seaweed in the rock-bound pools
Can justify Creation's rules.
The lobster, limpet, starfish, crab,
The whelk, the prawn, the plaice, the dab,
Yea, even purple jelly-fish,
That when you squeeze them only squish,
Illuminate the mind of man
In Nature's way and nature's plan.

This is a clever squib on the argument from design,[24] and as the Scopes Monkey Trial[25] was still fresh in everyone's mind, he wrote, in *Way Down in Tennessee*:

Oh, would I were in Tennessee,
The soil where all is fair and free,
Where man can never, never be
Descended from the apes...

A Child's Guide to Germany begins:

In speaking of the German, one
Notes the all-important fact
That he has ceased to be a Hun

---

[24] For the existence of God.
[25] In 1925, John T. Scopes, a schoolteacher, was tried for having taught human evolution, contrary to Tennessee law at the time.

Since signing the Locarno Pact[26].

A Child's Guide to Russia begins:

> The use of the explosive bomb
> Has rendered Russia different from
> The kindlier nations of the West;
> For always when he felt depressed
> And life appeared to lose its zest
> The Russian strove to cure his fits
> Of gloom by blowing things to bits.

Knox was the scion of a literary family, and his daughter, Penelope Fitzgerald, was a very distinguished novelist.

A.P. Herbert was another comic poet who had fought and been injured in the war, and he, too, wrote for *Punch* for many years, including during Knox's editorship. Melancholy and despair were not always absent from his work, but there was light-heartedness too:

> Yes, yes, the dentist talks a lot,
> For he's contented and you are not.
> He's the tiger in the house
> And you are, as it were, the mouse.

But like the other humourist, J.B. Morton, he published a serious novel in 1919 about the Great War, in which he served

---

[26] The Locarno Pact, 1925, normalised relations between Germany and France and Britain in return for a promise not to go to war again and to respect the then current European borders.

both at Gallipoli and on the Western Front. *The Secret Battle* is a short and powerful novel, considerably better from the purely literary point of view than Morton's. It recounts the story of Harry Penrose, a young subaltern who was a student at Oxford before joining up as an undergraduate. Like Herbert himself, he serves first in Gallipoli and then on the Western Front, exuding first a fanatical, almost mystical keenness that soon settles down to a grim determination to do his duty. In the end, after years of conspicuous bravery, he cracks under fire and is shot for cowardice—all by the age of twenty-three. The whole case against him is trumped up by a time-serving superior officer and a colleague who hates him because he, Harry Penrose, once observed his own real cowardice. The injustice is monstrous. The bone-headedness of the military tribunal and hierarchy that condemns him to death is in a way more terrifying than outright malignity would have been. The writing is controlled and the overall effect more powerful for an absence of shrillness.

Winston Churchill wrote a preface to the book. One might have thought that he would have wanted to avoid the subject of Gallipoli described in this book, the invasion of which had been his idea, even if the implementation was not his. The intense suffering of the fighting men is graphically described, and all is perfectly futile from the military point of view. The greatest victory of the whole campaign was the evacuation from the peninsula without further loss (in fact, the Turks may have lost more men than the British, French, Australians and New Zealanders, but the campaign was a blow to Allied prestige).

Churchill could absolve himself from blame for the disaster

by claiming, truly, that the operation was not carried out as he had conceived it, boldly rather than with caution. The top brass behaved with the same stupid punctilio as that with which they condemned Harry Penrose, delaying and prevaricating until the element of surprise was completely lost. But one might reply that Churchill ought to have taken the known characteristics of the commanders into account when he formed his scheme; otherwise, he is like a nineteenth century surgeon who claimed that the operation was a success, but the patient died.

Churchill praised the book generously, however uncomfortable the scenes in Gallipoli might have made him feel. In his preface, he recognises that Herbert was writing fiction but that all of it was realistic, in the way that a composite picture may be realistic. Not all the events in Harry Penrose's career may have happened to any one man, but all of them would have happened to someone. And indeed, Herbert knew of a young officer who was found guilty of cowardice and shot. This is life-changing knowledge.

In Gallipoli, Penrose falls sick. He suffers dysentery: 'The flesh seemed to have melted away from his face, and when he stood naked on the beach it seemed that the moving of his bones must soon tear holes in his unsubstantial skin.'

Penrose is seen by the doctor. 'And how do you feel now, Penrose?' he asks. 'All right, thank you, doctor,' he replies.

> The doctor looked at him queerly. He knew well enough, but it was his task to keep men on the Peninsula, not to send them away.

These days, of course, doctors are under the opposite pressure, to make people unfit for work to massage the government's unemployment statistics—and, of course, from the people themselves.

The following anecdote, surely taken from experience, brings home, if anything could, the horror of those days:

> … as we sat under a waterproof… there came an engineer officer wandering along the trench… 'Why don't you bury those Turks?' he said. 'They must have been there for weeks!' … we did not like the suggestion that those six good men of the 14th Platoon were dead Turks. We told him they were Englishmen, dead two hours. 'But, my God, man, they're black!' We led him back, incredulous, to the place.
>
> But when we got there, we understood. Whether from the explosion or the scorching sun in that airless place, I know not, but those six men were, as he said, literally black—black and reeking and hideous—and the flies…!

To write comic verse after this was probably the best way of healing a diseased memory, that is to say a memory diseased by what it truly remembered.

Herbert's book was eloquent on the subject of flies. 'Few more terrible plagues can have afflicted British troops than the flies of Gallipoli':

Most Englishmen have lain down some gentle summer day to doze on a shaded lawn and found one or two persistent flies have destroyed the repose of an afternoon... let them [average readers] for one fly imagine a hundred, a thousand, a million, and even then they will not exaggerate the horror of that plague.

In the year of Gallipoli, 1915, the eminent entomologist, Arthur Everett Shipley, master of Christ's College, Cambridge, and later vice-chancellor of the university, published a little book, *The Minor Horrors of War*, and a year later *More Minor Horrors*. I have both volumes, the former being a presentation copy by T.W. Kirkpatrick, author of *The Mosquitoes of Egypt*, of 1925, and *Insect Life in the Tropics*, of 1957, to the Natural History Society of his old school, Marlborough College. The minor horrors of the title are those animals, invertebrates, that prey on, inconvenience and spread disease to mankind. Minor horrors in themselves, they are instrumental in killing millions.

In his preface, Shipley says:

We are shy of mentioning these organisms in times of Peace; but all of them are within the cognisance of every medical officer of health... These gentlemen do not talk about them in general society: the subject as a rule is 'taboo'... I confess that these articles [the chapters in the book first published in the British Medical Journal] have been written in a certain spirit of gaiety. This is the reflex of the spirit of those who have gone to the Front and of my fellow country in general... Our nearest relatives, our dearest friends, are dead, or dying, or wounded, or prisoners, but we at home at once caught the spirit of those who have died or have suffered for us abroad, and we have kept and still keep a high heart. As Mrs. Aberdeen, the immortal 'bedmaker' at King's College, Cambridge, said, 'But surely, the world being what it is, the longer one is able to laugh at it, the better.' Mrs Aberdeen spoke in times of Peace: but I feel that the Indomitable old lady would have said the same in time of War.

We often laugh in retrospect, but I doubt that Herbert would ever have laughed heartily at the recollection of the flies of Gallipoli. And in fact, Shipley does not manage much levity about the housefly, the nearest he comes to levity being an anecdote about the famous motoring enthusiast, Lord Montagu of Beaulieu. Shipley writes:

Undoubtedly, the place most readily selected for the female for laying her eggs is stable-manure. A few years ago there was a remarkable reduction in the house-flies in London, and Lord Montagu of Beaulieu attributed this reduction to the refreshing and insecticidal petrol fumes with which the streets of that town were then bathed. I do not know what experiments Lord Montagu had made on the subject on the insecticidal virtue of petrol vapour, but the ordinary man in the street attributed—and I think more correctly—the diminution of the plague of flies to the absence of the nidus in which the female fly lays her eggs. Stable yards had been turned into garages.

Here is an aspect of social history of which I had not even thought: the prevalence of flies in summer.

In fact, Shipley does not make light of flies and says that their role in war is the spread of enteric diseases. He does not make mention of the torment that Herbert suffered in the year of his, Shipley's, book, for he could not have known of it at the time. But the effect of the advent of the motor car on the prevalence of flies (that advent having been an aesthetic disaster in a country as small and populated as England) was unsuspected by me. Perhaps the motor car brought with it a decline in enteric diseases also.

In the chapter on lice, Shipley says, 'As lice play a large part in the minor discomforts of an army, it is worth while considering for a moment what we know about them.' Since such lice spread typhus and in 1915 a typhus epidemic raged in Serbia that killed half the Serbian medical profession (as well as kept the Austrian army out of Serbia for a time), and as typhus killed two or three million people in the Russian Civil War, lice, I think, qualify as more than one of the minor horrors.

Still, Shipley's description of the means by which the life history of lice was illuminated in laboratories in Cambridge is fascinating. To know the life history, it was necessary to breed lice, which was far from easy. As Shipley puts it, 'When you want them to live, they die; and when you want them to die, they live, and multiply exceedingly.' In fact, we owe a deep debt to the people who intelligently and painstakingly investigated the life cycle of the minor horrors of war that we very rarely acknowledge.

We live freer of the kind of parasites that Shipley describes than any humans have lived before us. Because of my travels to less hygienic zones of the earth's surface, I have suffered from at least five of them, or four if one discounts the spread of malaria by mosquito. Unused to being parasitised in this way, I can confirm that when one *is* so parasitised, one is outraged, and it occupies the forefront of one's mind to the point of obsession. Once, for example, I had jiggers, the larvae of the sandflea, *Tunga penetrans*, that grow particularly between the toes. They are not themselves dangerous, but if not cleaned out carefully, can act as the port of entry of the tetanus germ. I once saw a man in Africa in the last stage of tetanus contracted via jiggers. The larvae had to be removed with a pin, ensuring that they were removed whole; if not, they became infected. But when one succeeded in removing them cleanly, they left a satisfyingly neat and painless hole in one's flesh that soon healed.

I caught scabies from a patient on a Pacific island with the so-called Norwegian form, that is to say fulminating and covering the whole body rather than the more usual form that burrows between the web of the fingers. Shipley says of the bed-bug, another of his minor horrors, that it is known by at least two scientific names, but the scabies mite has only one: *Sarcoptes scabei*.

In East Africa, I fell victim to the tumbu fly, *Cordylobia anthropophaga*, which lays its eggs in the creases of clothes and whose larvae burrow into the skin. I removed the growing maggots by covering the spiracles through which they breathed with Vaseline. They then emerged in their attempt to breathe. It was interesting to observe but reduced somewhat one's belief in the invariable beauty of nature.

I was once invaded by a tick, *Ixodes Ricinus*, and after removing it took medical advice as to whether I should take antibiotics prophylactically to prevent developing the disease that ticks can spread. The advice from the expert, no doubt based on the best scientific evidence available, was that I should not, but I took them all the same. The prospect of suffering a disease that was difficult to diagnose and treat was more real to me than any mere scientific evidence: rationality has its limits.

In his chapter on the parasite of cattle, the bot- or warble-fly, Shipley alludes to the shortage of medicinal leeches caused by the war, as if this were a considerable inconvenience, which in turn implies that the medicinal use of leeches was then still widespread. The bot-fly was a threat to leather supplies, the military demand for leather for army belts having exploded. Curiously enough, despite the prevalence of parasitism of cattle by the bot-fly, which drives them mad and weakens them, as well as ruining their skin for any useful purposes, the adult fly is rarely seen because it flies too fast for the eye to follow, and in 1916 there were very few examples in the entomological collections of the world.

Shipley wrote both to inform and amuse, making light of unpleasant phenomena to keep spirits up in dark times. The titles of his little books were humorous, jolly and misleading.

Curiously enough, Shipley mentions that the most important British economic entomologist of the late nineteenth century had been a woman, Miss Ormerod, on whose life Virginia Woolf wrote a short story eleven years after *The Minor Horrors of War*.

I must have been about nine or ten when I was first obliged to learn some lines of poetry by heart. They were by John Masefield, then still the Poet Laureate, and who had some years left to live. I do not have a good memory for poetry (I wish I did), but I remember:

> I must go down to the sea again, to the lonely sea and the skies,
> And all I ask is a tall ship and stars to steer her by…

Another of his poems that I learned was *Cargoes*:

> Stately Spanish galleon coming from the Isthmus,
> Dipping through the tropics by the palm-green shores,
> With a cargo of diamonds,
> Emeralds, amethysts,
> Topazes, and cinnamon, and gold moidores.

This somewhat romanticised account of the past contrasted with the ugly British present, then still industrialised:

> Dirty British coaster with a salt-caked smokestack,
> Butting through the Channel in the mad March days,
> With a cargo of Tyne coal,
> Road-rails, pig-lead,
> Firewood, iron-ware and cheap tin trays.

In 1916, Masefield, who had served as an ambulance man

on the Western Front, though his age had excused him from military service (which was not yet obligatory), wrote a book about the Gallipoli campaign, largely as a British propaganda effort in the United States, which of course had a large population of German origin potentially sympathetic to Germany. The failure of the Gallipoli campaign was of great value to the German cause, and according to Masefield, Germany put it about in the United States that the Ottomans had allowed the Allies to evacuate the peninsula in return for a bribe. The Germans wanted to make it look as if the United States would be joining a feeble and incompetent alliance if it sided with the Allies. Masefield's book, titled *Gallipoli*, makes no mention of the contemporary Armenian massacres.

There is evidence enough in the book of incompetence of the Gallipoli campaign. For it to have succeeded, it would have had either to be a complete surprise or carried out with overwhelming force. In the event, it was neither a surprise nor carried out with enough men and materiel. (It was Churchill who suggested that 50,000 men should be sufficient, but he also advocated surprise.)

My copy of the book once belonged to George Van Santvoord, who was an American Rhodes scholar at Oxford in 1916 who bought the book in the week of its publication and inscribed it in his elegant script. His script was so elegant that it was mentioned in an obituary of him published in 1975.

I do not think that Van Santvoord was, despite his erudition, a name known to history, but he was an estimable and honourable man. Born in 1891, he attended the Hotchkiss School, a private institution in Connecticut of which he later became headmaster, from 1926 to 1955. After taking a B. Lit. at Oriel College, he served as an ambulance driver for the French army, and when America joined the war, he served in the 39th Infantry Division, winning the *Croix de Guerre*. After the war, he taught literature at Yale and was professor of literature at the University of Buffalo until he was appointed headmaster of his old school. He was by all accounts a disciplinarian but one with the obituary writer's obligatory warm heart. 'He saw the school through the Great Depression, the Second World War, and the Korean War, upholding the highest standards of academic excellence.' Now the school proudly boasts on its website that 37 per cent of its students (not *pupils*, nota bene) are people of colour, though of which colour is not further specified. Humanity is divided into whites and people of colour.

In his book, Masefield tries to make the best of a bad job: 'That the effort [of the Gallipoli landing] failed is not against it; much that is most splendid in military history failed, many great things noble men have failed.' This seems to me to rely on a *non sequitur*, as follows:

Many noble endeavours have failed.

This endeavour failed.

Therefore, this endeavour was noble.

The British, it seems, have a special affection for failure, as indeed do I. They love figures like Captain Scott who failed to reach the South Pole or who reached it only after Amundsen. (Amundsen cheated by his superior knowledge and planning.) I have a fellow-feeling with failures.

Masefield did not go to Gallipoli and doesn't mention how he came by his information. He doesn't disguise the horrors, including the flies, which he says were so numerous that they resembled patches of bootblack. He attributed their numbers to the dirtiness of 'the Turk', the Allied camps being much cleaner, though he also says that chronic dysentery was universal in them—the amoebic rather than the bacterial kind. He has, as one would expect, a poetic imagination, though there can have been few more difficult subjects for poetry than the Gallipoli landing seen from afar. Here he describes the advance—not very far—of the Allied troops on the peninsula:

Those watchers [the defending Turks] saw the dotted order of our advance stretching across the Peninsula, moving slowly forward, and halting and withering away, among fields of flowers of spring, and the young corn that would never come to harvest. They saw the hump of Achi Baba [a prominent hill] flicker and burn up to heaven in a swathe of blindness, and multitudinous brightness changing the face of the earth, and dots of our line still coming, still moving forward, and halting and withering away, but still moving up among the flashes and darkness, more men, and yet more men, from the fields of sacred France, from the darkness of Senegal, from sheep-runs at the end of the earth [i.e. New Zealand], from blue-gum forests [i.e. Australia], and sunny islands, places of horses and good fellows, from Irish pastures and glens, and from many a Scotch and English city and village and quiet farm; they went on and they went on[27],

---

[27] A little like Masefield.

up ridges blazing with explosion into the darkness of death...

What kept them going, I wonder (assuming they did keep going)? Belief in their cause, as the Turks and Germans believed in their cause? The obloquy of being thought cowardly? Or had they seen and experienced such things that death itself seemed a possible relief from them? I think that the fact that we could not fight in the same way today has both a good and a bad aspect: the good being that we value men's lives more highly, the bad being that we don't have anything we believe is worth dying for. The nearest we come to have anything worth dying for is an exceptionally delicious dish: 'It is to die for.'

By the time Gallipoli was evacuated, it was winter. Having endured terrible blazing heat, the troops were now frozen:

> Before the night fell, many of our men were frost-bitten and started limping to the ambulances, under continual shrapnel fire and in blinding sleet. A good many fell down by the way, and were frozen to death... The 28th [November] was spoken ever afterward as "Frozen Feet Day"; it was a day more terrible than any battle.

There was one advantage to it, however:

> Either the cold or the rain destroyed the cause of dysentery, which had taken nearly a thousand victims a day for some months.

We must always look on the bright side of things.

I will try not to write about the First World War, or typhus, for much longer, but simply because I have it in my possession, I will mention *Typhus Fever with Particular Reference to the Serbian Epidemic*, by Richard P. Strong *et al.*, published in 1920 by the Harvard University Press, rather expensively done. How, or even why, I came by it, I cannot now recall, except to say that the history of epidemics has always interested me and was for long a relatively neglected subject. One of the authors of this volume, Hans Zinsser, professor of bacteriology at Columbia College, later wrote a very famous book, *Rats, Lice and History*, reprinted many times, which was an early account of the part played in history by epidemics and which now seems so obvious to us—now that epidemics are few and far between—but which did not always seem so obvious. Hume, for example, in his *History of England*, gives the Black Death only passing mention, though it killed perhaps a third of the population. I once read a standard history of Colonial Guatemala that failed to mention that the population declined by ninety per cent in the century after the conquest thanks to the epidemic diseases such as smallpox and measles new to the population, to which it had had no previous exposure, that the Spanish brought with them. I suspect that the author failed to mention these rather important facts because they did not accord with his view that there was human motivation, ultimately economic, behind all history.

We have, of course, recently been forcibly reminded of the

181

importance of epidemics, and more particularly of the importance of our response to them. Almost everyone is now certain that what was done during the Covid epidemic was wrong, and some claim always to have known it; and of course, we all know what to do next time, though the next time might be very different. But even at its worst, the Covid epidemic was nothing like the Serbian typhus epidemic of 1915 (when my father was six years old).

Dr Strong, the first author of *Typhus Fever*, was head of the American Red Cross Commission in Serbia (America had not yet become a belligerent in the war). He says that of 350 Serbian doctors, the great majority of them had contracted the disease and 126 of them had died of it:

> Of the thirteen physicians in the hospital at Pirot [one of the first Dr Strong visited on his arrival in the country], twelve contracted the disease and six died of it.

Conditions in the hospital, not surprisingly, were dreadful, especially considering that the disease was spread by lice and lice were spread by intimate contact. 'Indeed, it was exceptional in most of the hospitals to find only one patient in a bed, usually there were three or four patients in a bed and the available floor space was also covered with patients without beds; sometimes lying on straw, on blankets, or closely huddled side by side on the wooden flooring, often even under the beds.' They received no attention since there was no one to give it. Of 70,000 Austrian prisoners of war, 35,000 died of typhus. Captain Bennett, of the British Red Cross, described a prison camp for Austrians:

It is not a hospital... but simply where 750 Austrians have been collected... At an earlier date one doctor was in charge of this camp, but he is now stricken down with typhus, and various forms of the infection are raging unchecked. Typhus, dysentery, smallpox, and diphtheria have swept over the place with devastating effects. Last week, only twenty men out of 750 could stand on their feet... The silence of the camp is broken only by sighs and groans. A recent visitor noticed a number of recumbent forms covered with greatcoats and found on removing these that five out of their number had already been dead several days.

One hospital was so bad that 'It is practically impossible to go near it; so overpowering is the stench of the street outside that nobody who is not compelled to approach the building can bear to be in its vicinity. Details of the interior cannot well be printed.'

The international commission to control the epidemic in Serbia seems to have been successful, or at any rate the epidemic came to an end. Among the methods employed was a disinfecting train:

The efficacy of the sanitary disinfecting train units we employed in Serbia was due particularly to the chief engineer of the Serbian railway service who displayed considerable ingenuity in directing the conversion of the cars for this purpose. As employed by us in Serbia these sanitary train units consisted of three cars, one of which was occupied by a large engine boiler for supplying the steam; a second car, a large refrigerator one, was made air tight, felt being placed at the edge of the side door, and a connecting steam pipe was so arranged that steam from the boiler could be turned into it under low pressure, the ordinary system of pipes in the roof of these cars, finely perforated, being also thus connected up with the boiler engine. The clothing was hung loosely in the car on a wire suspended from hooks. Both lice and ova on the clothing was killed in a very few minutes in this manner... In a third car there were shower baths and a reservoir for water above.

What perhaps is surprising, given that most of them must have been peasants with little conception or understanding of infectious disease, was that most Serbians were very trusting— but of course, the Second World War had not yet taken place, with its shower baths employed for another purpose.

The people marched... several hundred at a time. Usually their hair was clipped, and then, after undressing, the clothing was placed in the steam sterilizing car. They next passed to the car in which the shower baths were placed, and after a thorough scrubbing with soap and water, they were sprayed with kerosene as an additional precaution.

Then their clothes were returned to them, or they were given new clothes.

Did they accept this willingly, knowingly, joyfully, or were they coerced into compliance? They could hardly have been *au fait* with the latest medical doctrine. The book does not ask the question, let alone answer it. The photographs of the railway carriages concerned looked very sinister to me, but I have a post-World-War-II sensibility. Did the Germans get any of their subsequent ideas from these sanitary trains? Serbia, it is said, lost more of its population, proportionately, than any other country during the First World War. It is estimated that between 150,000 and 350,000 people were lost to typhus alone, three per cent of the whole population. In a sense it hardly matters which, and in another sense, it matters a great deal. Our minds cannot easily encompass such things, each death being a tragedy.

It is surely time for something a little lighter: but the trouble is that, when I study my bookshelves, I find very little that could be called humorous. When I see a section in a bookshop marked 'Humour', I avoid it.

Furthermore, my books are not classified by anything except size, rather like the Suras of the Koran. There could be no section, therefore, for funny books, which tend not to be large or long. But between *A Briefe and Accurate Treatise Concerning the Taking of Tobacco Which very many in these days doe too licentiously use*, by Tobias Venner, printed and published in 1650, and *Forward from Liberalism*, a somewhat bloodcurdling call for communism by Stephen Spender, published in 1937 (by the time I met him decades later, he had become an amiable and grand old man of letters, knighted and full of honours), I found a slender red volume with the title *Robert's*

Wife. Advertised on the cover as a comedy in three acts by St, John Ervine. Something titled a comedy ought to hold out the hope, at least, of laughter.

First performed in 1937, my copy of the play was printed in 1946, and I must have bought it many years ago, attracted to it as I was by the fact that it bore the signatures of the Frodsham Players, an amateur dramatic society still in existence. As I knew nothing of Ervine, not even that he had existed, I must have bought the book for an extraneous reason: for I would have assumed that a dramatist of whom I had not heard could not have been very good.[28]

Nearby on the shelf was a genuine work of humour, albeit of the black kind, with illustrations, titled *Ruthless Rhymes for Heartless Homes* by Harry Graham[29], first published in 1898. My copy is a very early edition and some of the black and white illustrations have been quite skilfully water-coloured by a previous owner. The rhymes are indeed of a ruthlessness which would have made a certain kind of boy—of whom I was one—squeal with delight. Here is one of the least ruthless:

> Father, chancing to chastise
> His indignant daughter, Sue,
> Said, "I hope you realise
> That this hurts me more than you?"
>
> Susan straightway ceased to roar:

---

[28] It is astonishing how much of one's own life one must deduce from the evidence, as if writing a biography of a third party.
[29] Harry Graham, 1874-1936, was an English humourist, army officer, poet and journalist.

"If that's really true," said she,
"I can stand a good deal more;
Pray go on and don't mind me."

I suppose you could say that there was a serious point to this, namely the exposure of the hypocrisy of those who enjoy beating children supposedly for their own good.

But to return to St John Ervine's play, the comedy in three acts, *Robert's Wife*. I had expected something light and frivolous, Noel Coward without the wit, perhaps, but on the contrary the play was nearer to tragedy than to comedy, except in the sense that the whole of life is a comedy, though it contained one or two lines that were mildly amusing rather than wildly funny.

The play takes place in the sitting room of a vicarage in an industrial town in the South of England.[30] The Reverend Robert Carson is married to Sanchia, a doctor, who runs a medical clinic in the town, including a birth control department. In 1937, birth control was still considered a controversial subject, regarded by its opponents as an invitation to licentiousness and by its proponents as a means of alleviating child poverty consequent upon the bearing of many children in quick succession and of bettering the life of women.

Robert's son, Bob, is at Oxford, and a communist, 'of course'. He is also a militant pacifist and, with the moral certainty of a twenty-year-old, goes to a military camp nearby to encourage soldiers to desert. He is arrested for sedition and

---

[30] Presumably light rather than heavy industry.

sentenced to a year in prison.

His father, meanwhile, is in the running to be raised to a nearby deanery (I suppose the ecclesiastic equivalent of a colonelcy) but the activities of his son, together with his wife's advocacy of birth control, put his appointment at risk. A rich but not very bright widow, whose husband made a fortune from the manufacture of artificial milk, initially thinks of donating five thousand pounds—a large sum in those days— to Sanchia's clinic but withdraws the offer when Sanchia insists on promoting birth control and Bob goes to prison.

The play is very well-constructed and, with the exception of the rich widow and a rigid Anglo-Catholic priest, Arthur Jefferson, who does all he can to raise objections to Sanchia's clinic, all the characters are sympathetic without being stereotyped or uninteresting. St John Ervine, my ignorance of him notwithstanding, was a successful and prolific playwright, much admired by W.B. Yeats, Bernard Shaw and Sean O'Casey. It takes, I repeat, great skill to interest us in good people.

I doubt that the play could be put on successfully now because the salience of the dilemmas of the characters would be lost on us, so different has life become, and so limited are our efforts to enter the worlds of others (while we play lip-service to multiculturalism, of course). Who can now remember when anyone other than conservative Catholics denounced birth control? As for communism or pacifism, neither is now very strongly believed in. When Bob meets the local bishop, who at 67 is described by the author in his stage directions as old, he says to him, when he learns that the Bishop is going to preach to the troops in the nearby army camp, 'You're not going to praise war, are you?' To which the bishop, a wise old bird, replies, 'I shan't praise it, Bob. I had three sons when the last one began. I hadn't any when it was over. I don't think I shall praise war. But I won't refuse my blessing to men who are willing to die for what they think is a good cause.'

Especially in hindsight, we sympathise more with the Bishop than with Bob (how much grief is conjured by the Bishop's simple words!). Interestingly, the foreign bogeyman in the play—remember that it is 1937—is Mussolini, mentioned several times, and not Hitler, who is not once mentioned.

The incipient degeneration of the Church of England can be sensed, perhaps unintentionally, in the play. The vicar is dynamic and go-ahead, and in retrospect, destructive. 'If I were Dean,' says the Reverend Carson, 'I'd try to make the old cathedral of ours a working church, instead of a picturesque relic of the Middle Ages. There it stands in the close, the loveliest thing in the city, and the most dead.'

One can all but sense in these words the coming of the plastic stackable chairs, the strumming of guitars, the playpen and the posters asking for contributions to combat trachoma in Africa. They reminded me of my brief time in Rotherham, a now-dismal town in which the loveliest thing by far was the Minster, a fifteenth century Perpendicular-Gothic church adapted to modern needs by a plywood kitchen from which cups of tea could be dispensed to old people, the nearest thing the Church of England can come to making a church work or a place of frequentation.

As I mentioned, the book must have attracted me because

of the signatures of the cast, with the parts in the play that they acted. I looked up one on the internet, Rowland Shelbourne, on the off-chance that there was something about him to be found there. I chose him because his signature was both refined and full of self-confidence. This is what I found:

> Two councillors have revealed they were the victims of sexual abuse at the hands of their primary school headteacher… at a Frodsham Town Council meeting when they spoke publicly of the abuse they were subjected to by Overton Church of England head Rowland Shelbourne in the 1950s. They believe that they were just two of the schoolchildren who were abused by Mr Shelbourne, who died in 1974. He was also head at Manor Croft Infant School from 1965. A leading figure in Frodsham, he helped found the community centre and was a special police constable.
>
> One of the councillors said, "It was the 1950s and it wasn't anything anyone talked about, though everyone in the school knew it was going on."

A plaque to the headmaster in the Town Hall was removed because a large number of people requested it. 'The people who made these requests feel extremely strongly about it. One even told us that they (*sic*) felt physically sick every time they (*sic*) walked past [it].'

Sherbourne played Jefferson, one of the two dislikable characters in the play, the rigid, almost theocratic clergyman. Shelbourne's wife, Bertha, played Sanchia, the Reverend Robert Carson's wife. Her signature, less forceful than his, appears above his name. I felt glad that the revelations were made only after her death—for I am sure that by that time, she was dead.

Attentive readers, if any, will recall that in the section on the minor horrors of war, I mentioned a Miss Ormerod: I do not wish to imply that she was one of the minor horrors. On the contrary, she was a most estimable lady, the first woman ever to have an honorary doctorate conferred on her by the University of Edinburgh. I mentioned also that Virginia Woolf wrote a short story about her, a kind of potted biography. It was an undistinguished piece of work, and I think it might, if read on its own, leave the reader a little mystified—which, perhaps, was the intention, many people mistaking mystification for depth.

At any rate, Mrs Woolf had the honesty to admit that she derived most of her information, insofar as her story was documentary, from *Eleanor Ormerod, Economic Entomologist: Autobiography and Correspondence*, edited by Robert Wallace, who was professor of agriculture and rural economy in the University of Edinburgh.

In fact, the book is mostly of her letters, though at the beginning are some of her recollections. They are curious for their complete impersonality. The only real warmth she ever expresses is for her older sister, who died before her and helped her in her entomological work, being a fine illustrator of insects. (Eleanor Ormerod was a gifted draughtswoman also, a fact not mentioned in Mrs Woolf's story, nor the fact that she was a gifted linguist, able to correspond in Russian, for example, surely not a commonplace accomplishment at the time, or indeed today).

Included in Mrs Woolf's story is an anecdote from Miss Ormerod's reminiscences. She was the youngest of ten children whose father was the owner of Sedbury Park, a very large house in Gloucestershire. Early in her life, she was left to amuse herself in the house while everyone else went out for a walk and did so by observing the larvae of a water beetle in a jar. One of the larvae died while she was watching, and the other larvae ate it. When her father and the others returned home from their walk, she told them excitedly what she had seen: but her father pooh-poohed it and would hear no more of it. She had to keep silent.

This put me in mind of two episodes from my own life. I must have been about nine when I saw a fox in our garden in London, and when I told my father, he said I must have imagined it, for it was impossible. But in the not very distant future, foxes in England became more numerous in towns than in the country. Be that as it may, I learned a certain confidence in my own judgment and a mistrust in that of others when it contradicted my own. This led me to become an intolerable know-all.

The second episode happened in Switzerland, when I was of about the same age. We were rowing close to the shore of Lake Lugano when I spotted there a dark snake with a yellow ring around its neck. It was shy and skittered away immediately. I recounted what I had seen but again was told that I was imagining it. What I saw, however, corresponded exactly to descriptions of *Natrix helvetica*, a grass snake that is dark in colour and has a yellow band around its neck, another specimen of which I saw sixty years later on my property in France.

Miss Ormerod was a more interesting figure than Mrs Woolf's short but nevertheless dull story-cum-essay makes her out to have been. Although it was very unusual for a woman in her time to make a mark on science, Miss Ormerod was no feminist. After a lecture that she gave to a crowded Richmond Athenaeum:

> Miss Lydia Becker, at that time a vigorous upholder of "Women's Rights", rose to speak, and while praising Miss Ormerod's able lecture, instanced her work as being "a proof of how much a woman could do without the help of a man." Miss Ormerod, in her reply, thanked Miss Becker, but begged to say that she had no right to the praise accorded to her the ground of her work being so entirely that of a lone woman, for, she said, "No one owes more to the help of man than myself. I have always met with the greatest kindness and most generous aid from my friends of the other sex, and without their constant encouragement my poor efforts would have had no practical result in being of benefit to my fellow men."

No one would speak in this fashion today, and I daresay no woman would refer to 'my fellow men'. Miss Ormerod was, of course, extremely fortunate in her social class: she never had to worry about money and indeed subsidised her own publications on insect pests, agricultural and horticultural, of which she became a pre-eminent expert and of world renown.

(She gave testimony in court cases into such matters as the insect degradation of imported flour, and I note that even in those days cases were settled out of court when the litigation was of no merit, it being more expensive to prove it than to pay something to the litigant to go away).

Like Virginia Woolf, Miss Ormerod never had to cope with the boring domestic details of daily life; but it must be remembered to the credit of both, but particularly of Miss Ormerod, that plenty of women were in a similar economic situation, but very few achieved anything like as much.

As it happens, however, there was one such lady who lived not very far from where in England I write this. Her name was Frances Pitt, and she was of more or less the same social class as Miss Ormerod. Their lives overlapped in time slightly: Miss Pitt would have been thirteen when Miss Ormerod died.[31]

Frances Pitt was born in a large house in the countryside of Shropshire and, like Miss Ormerod, very early became enamoured of natural history. Like her, she had no formal schooling, except by private tutors, and was free to roam in the countryside. She became not only one of the most popular writers on nature in the country—she wrote a weekly column in the London *Evening News* for thirty-five years, well within my lifetime—but a serious entomologist who published the results of her researches in *Nature* (no higher accolade is possible) and some of her many books on animal behaviour are still worth reading. She kept otters, foxes, badgers, crows and red squirrels (among other animals) at home, and the present owner of the house, who kindly showed me in, told me

---

[31] Eleanor Ormerod 1820-1901, Frances Pitt 1888-1964.

that when she lifted the floorboards of the attic, she discovered nuts hidden there by squirrels sixty or seventy years before.

Like Miss Ormerod, she never married (or had any financial difficulties). A proposal to place a plaque in her honour in the nearby town was opposed because she had also been Master of the Hunt and wrote a book about fox-hunting. This was so strongly disapproved of that it more than cancelled out her other great achievements, though the hunt in her days had been an important part of the social calendar. No understanding or concession is to be extended to those benighted enough to have lived in the past.

Reading the book about and by Miss Ormerod brought back another memory. She refers in it to *Army Worm*, the kind of caterpillar that, having undergone a population explosion, marches in a very long and wide column and consumes everything in its path. I think I may fairly say that I have been one of the few cricketers whose match had to be abandoned because of the arrival on the pitch (in Africa) of Army Worm.

Miss Ormerod, unexpectedly, had something in common with Mao Tse-Tung: she, like him, was a ferocious enemy of the sparrow. This is a subject to which I will immediately turn.

William Berhardt Tegetmeier, of German ancestry but British nationality, was a doctor who became more interested in bees than in people and was a friend of Charles Darwin. Like Miss Ormerod and Mao Tse-Tung, he was an enemy of the house sparrow and in 1899 published a little book titled *The House Sparrow (The Avian Rat)*. No one, I think, compares anything to a rat in complimentary fashion.

My copy of the little book has one of the nastiest bookplates I have ever seen, a design of a green colour that manages somehow to combine brightness with dullness, of a disturbingly asymmetrical design. I will not dishonour the memory of the dead by revealing whose it was.

Tegetmeier was Miss Ormerod's ally in the war against the sparrow, hoping to reduce its numbers if not to extirpate it entirely. To me, the house sparrow is merely a cheeky little bird that flies in and out of the bushes in my front garden and the gardens of my neighbours. Apparently, though, I should not feel so indulgent towards it. Appended to the book is Miss Oremerod's and Dr Tegetmeier's pamphlet on the subject of the house sparrow, of which the former had 36,000 copies printed at her own expense and distributed for free. That is sincere belief for you.

If I had the means to print 36,000 copies of a pamphlet and hand them out, or post them, for free, one what subject, for or against, would they be? So many things irritate me: chewing gum, tattooing, ugly dogs, fat people in tight clothes, vapes, beer in cans rather than in bottles. The list is practically endless. The house sparrow, though, wouldn't be in it.

Tegetmeier writes as if the little bird were to blame for its own nature. The counts against it are almost as many as those against Donald Trump in courts in Democrat states. For example, the house sparrow drives away other birds, especially useful insectivorous ones such as swifts and martins.

> Yarell [the English ornithologist]... reports the old story of the housemartins having revenged themselves by

walling up their enemy alive, and leaving him to die [in a martin's nest] a prisoner in the domicile he has violated.

But however much Tegetmeier might have liked to believe this story, he does not credit it:

> That twenty or thirty martins should combine together for the purpose of plastering up a sparrow in a nest is too improbable a circumstance to be believed, except on the most incontrovertible evidence: and that a sparrow, with its strong and powerful beak should sit quietly in a nest while the martins were plastering it up is too incredible a statement to be accepted, in spite of the fact that Macgillivray himself, one of the most observant of naturalists, recounts it—not, however, from his own observations, but from statements that were related to him by persons who were not naturalists.

This, in essence, is Hume's argument against the reality of miracles, that they are to be accepted only when it is less likely that the observers of them were mistaken than that they occurred—a condition that is never satisfied. Therefore, there are no miracles.

The main fault of the sparrow is that it is graminivorous and does great harm to the agriculture which is carried out within a short distance of the towns in which they live, also destroying urban gardens and vegetable patches. I must say that we have both many sparrows and a flourishing garden, but I suppose that this is not a conclusive argument against Tegetmeier. At any rate, the latter and Miss Ormerod base themselves on an analysis carried out on the contents of sparrows' stomachs, from which it was concluded that three quarters of their diet is of grain. They also love ripe peas.

It is true, they say, that fledgeling sparrows are brought up on insect grubs, and that this had been used as a defence of the usefulness of birds (insects then being the enemy), but analysis also showed that the kind of grubs upon which they were brought up were of the agriculturally and horticulturally harmless type.

The defenders of the house sparrow need very little refutation, says Tegetmeier and Miss Ormerod, so feeble are their arguments. Some of those arguments were Biblical: but even here Tegetmeier says they are mistaken. The Hebrew name *tzippot* does not mean sparrow, but little bird of any kind. And the defenders of sparrows get their natural history all wrong. Edith Carrington, a vociferous critic of Miss Ormerod's anti-sparrovianism, to coin a word, claimed that sparrows are beneficial because they destroy cockchafers, which are their favourite food, both the grub and the imago. But Miss Carrington 'is obviously ignorant of the fact that the grubs of the cockchafer inhabit the ground in which the sparrow cannot pick, and that the mature insect flies about only at night, after the sparrows, which are the earliest birds to retire, have gone to roost.' Tegetmeier refers to further absurdities such that sparrows have been found so gorged with grubs of May bugs as to be unable to fly—the grubs of May bugs being inaccessible to sparrows in any case. Moreover, the defenders of sparrows are inconsistent when they refer to sparrows as God's children: this being the case, so is the rattlesnake.[32]

Tegetmeier has a detailed chapter, titled *Diminishing the Sparrow Plague*, on sparrow traps of various designs, and points out that sparrows are good eating—being of a certain class, he did not have to worry about the labour involved in plucking them. He says that they are an adornment to any steak and kidney pie. Having learned this, I am not sure that I shall ever watch the little birds twittering round the bushes in my garden in quite the same way again.

In the late 19th Century there were many sparrow clubs formed by landowners large and small. Members paid a subscription and if they failed to capture a certain number of sparrows every month, they paid a fine which would be used at the end of the year for a supper for all the members. The author is delicately silent about how the birds were to be killed, but each member had to provide the heads of the sparrows that he had killed to a designated member of the club for verification. Naturally, the heads of other birds were not acceptable and did not count. As Miss Ormerod and Mr Tegetmeier put it at the end of their pamphlet:

> We believe that subscription, whether local or from those who know the desirableness of aiding in the work of endeavouring to save the bread of the people from these feathered robbers, would be money wisely and worthily

---

[32] Though fifteen of the twenty most venomous snakes in the world are found in Australia, they are protected by law. It is said that 7,000 people a year in Bangladesh are killed by Russell's viper alone.

spent.

The authors put the economic loss to farmers and horticulturalists at the hands, or rather the wings and beaks, of sparrows at between 1 and 2 million pounds annually, that is to say between 100 and 200 million in today's money.

Mao Tse-Tung was another fervent sparrow exterminator—but then, he didn't mind exterminating people, either.

We stopped off in Stroud, in Gloucestershire, Miss Ormerod's county, on our way to the village of Bisley, where there was to be a memorial cricket match for my friend, John Mortimer Cobbe, who died after a long illness on Christmas day, 2023.

He was my friend for more than forty years, and the most equable person I ever knew. As Falstaff was not only witty in himself but the cause of wit in others, so John was not only equable in himself, but the cause of equability in others. To be unruffled as an anaesthetist (for such he was) is an important professional quality, but he carried it over from the professional to the private sphere, which is not always the case. His equability, and equanimity, which nobody ever saw him lose, was not mere blindness to the wickedness or sufferings of the world. In addition, his last years, alas, were of great suffering, but he bore it patiently and it never undermined his character.

When he was still well, he arranged a cricket match once a year, for twenty years, on Bisley's beautiful village ground, between his selected team and the village team. This fixture ceased when he could play no more, about fifteen years ago. I was of his eleven, in which I played an enthusiastic but very minor part. His widow decided on a memorial game (their sons being both good players), but fortunately it was not expected that I should play. My last village game had been about three years before and it nearly killed me.

It was a fine day and, as the cliché has it, a good time was had by all. Gnawing away at the back of my mind was the question of whether we should be enjoying ourselves in the name of one so recently (just over six months) dead, but he would have wanted it thus: it was no part of his character to spread dolefulness, and he took every opportunity to enjoy life.

Before arriving in Bisley, as I have said, we stopped off in Stroud where an artist of my acquaintance had an exhibition to which I had promised to go if I could. A few yards from the gallery was that increasing rarity, a good second-hand bookshop, to which I flew like a fly to ordure. I had little time at my disposal, for my wife was waiting in the car which was parked where it shouldn't have been parked; I had to be very disciplined, for time flies for me in such a bookshop, and an hour passes for me in seconds.

I alighted at once, in the poetry section, on a little volume bound in dark green, *The Poems of Mary E. Coleridge*. I had not heard of her, but I assumed that she was of the Coleridge family. So it proved, and she had modestly refused to publish her poems under her own name during her lifetime for fear of soiling that illustrious name and lineage. Her fear, I think, was unjustified. She reminded me, though on a somewhat lower plane, of the greatest of American poets, Emily Dickinson.

Mary E. Coleridge was religious but with that kind of mysticism which one does not have to be religious to understand or appreciate; to do so one has only to be aware that a mystery remains at the heart of human existence—as I for one hope that always will be.

As soon as I opened the book and read one or two of her short poems—she wrote no long ones—I realised that she suited my mood of guilty melancholy (melancholy that my friend had died, guilt that I continued my life as before as if unaffected by his death, and that, if I had *really* been his friend, I should have been affected for the rest of my life). Was I, then, a bad friend?

This is a question that has pursued me (mildly, if a pursuit can be mild) throughout my life. I remember the death of my dog, the being that I loved most in the world, when I was still a child, and how, for some time afterwards, I felt compelled to rise from my warm comfortable bed, against my wishes, to touch the ceiling: failure to do which repeatedly would have been proof of the insufficiency or insincerity of my love for him. I did all this without the slightest belief in life after death, or expectation that I would meet him again after my own demise.

But to return to Mary E. Coleridge, great-grand-niece to Samuel Taylor, whose poems were published under her own name in 1908, the year after her death at the age of 46 of septicaemia contracted after an operation for appendicitis. Her work reminded me, in content, form and sensibility, of that of Emily Dickinson's, which she could not have known— a case of convergent literary evolution. Here, for example, is her poem, *Doubts*:

Two forms of darkness are there. One is Night,
When I have been an animal, and feared
I know not what, and lost my soul, nor dared
Feel aught save hungry longing for the light.
And one is Blindness. Absolute and bright,
The Sun's rays smote me till they masked the Sun;
The Light itself was by the light undone.
The day was filled with terrors and affright.

This is not very far from Emily Dickinson's simplicity of diction and profundity of feeling:

Tell all the truth, but tell it slant –
Success in Circuit lies
Too bright for our infirm Delight
The Truth's superb surprise
As Lightning to the Children eased
With explanation kind
The Truth must dazzle gradually
Or every man be blind—

Mary E. Coleridge ends her poem:

Then did I weep, compassionate of those
Who see no friend in God—in Satan's host no foes.

I think her compassion real for those poor souls such as I who see no purpose or design in existence and cannot persuade themselves that there is one just because it would be more comfortable to believe in one. By this, I do not mean to imply that Mary E. Coleridge's faith was anything other than genuine and was not mere wishful thinking.

I know almost nothing of her biography, but her poetry seems to suggest a good, sensitive, kind, loving but unfulfilled person, who, despite her membership of a privileged class, even caste, knew great suffering:

> None ever was in love with me but grief.
> > She wooed me from the day that I was born,
> She stole my playthings first, the jealous thief,
> > And left me there forlorn.

I sense, though I cannot prove, that this is not exaggeration, no mere exercise in romantic emotional exhibitionism (such as I suspect her great-great uncle, or Sylvia Plath, to have indulged in). Thus, when she writes:

> Tired of the daily round,
> > And tired of all my being;
> My ears are tired with sound,
> > And mine eyes with seeing...

I do not roll my eyes up with the exaggeration of it all: there is such a thing as *taedium vitae*. I feel it temporarily when confronted by the boring tasks of everyday life, such as the completion of tax forms; but it can be chronic, and I have to pinch myself to remember that Mary E. Coleridge was at least thirty years younger than I am now when she wrote the above. People aged more quickly in those days, however.

My friend in Bisley suffered so much that I think he would

have been glad to die—as I would not yet be glad. But as I walk in the small town where I am known to some, I almost always think, 'This will all be the same the very day after my death; the butcher will open as usual, the greengrocer, the wine merchant etc. Life will close over me as the water of a pond closes over a pebble thrown into it.' Am I glad or sad of it? Let Mary E. Coleridge decide:

> When I am dead, I know that thou wilt weep,
>> I that never caused thee grief before...

> When I am dead I know thou wilt forget,
>> Thou that didst never yet forget a friend.

When Salman Rushdie was attacked by an assailant with a knife in Chautauqua, New York, I was truly appalled. The assailant struck Rushdie fifteen times, most horrifyingly in the eye. For some reason, that last blow was particularly appalling, an attack not so much on the body as on the soul (of which the eyes are normally a mirror). I do not know whether the assailant aimed it to be, but so it was in effect.

I had not much regard for Rushdie as a writer—his writing always struck me as forced and exhibitionistic—but V.S. Naipaul's joke, that the Ayatollah's fatwa upon him was literary criticism of unusual severity, while funny, was not in the best of taste. A man who is under threat of death for what he has written deserves our support rather than our snide remarks.[33] To live so long under the threat of death, like an American prisoner on death row, and then to seem to be free of it, only to become the victim of such an attack, as stupid as it was brutal, is not something endured by many of us, and entitles Rushdie to our sympathy and support.

Still, I can't think of him as a good writer. He is to Gabriel García Marquez what Little Venice in Maida Vale in London is to Venice in Italy, or perhaps as Dr Thorndyke is to Sherlock Holmes. I read Rushdie's memoir of the knife attack upon him and thought it good only in parts—small parts at that.

Rushdie says in his memoir that he does not want to use the name of his assailant, and I can well understand this. To name him would be in some sense to do him honour, which he does not deserve, so Rushdie simply calls him *A*. He writes:

> I do not want to use his name in this account. My Assailant, my would-be Assassin, the Asinine man who made Assumptions about me, and with whom I had a near-lethal Assignation—I have found myself thinking of him, perhaps forgivably, as an Ass.[34]

I cannot say what effect this passage has on others, but on

---

[33] I once had a discussion with some young people about an extraordinarily crude and vulgar comedian, who made very nasty jokes. 'But he's funny,' they protested. I did not find him so; he was merely coarse. But even if I had found him funny, I should not have excused him on those grounds.

[34] Whether Rushdie is here using the word *ass* in its British sense (a stupid animal) or in its American sense (an anus), or perhaps both, I cannot say.

me it indicates a man trying to be clever, to be witty without truly being so. I may be doing the writer an injustice, for I must keep in mind his suffering, but he seems to me here to be showing off merely. The nearest he comes to wit is when he talks of the foreshadowing in his books of the knife attack: 'I've had some trouble with prophets in my life, and I'm not applying for the job.' This made me laugh.

Sometimes, his writing is inexact, as in the following:

> On such coin-toss moments a life can turn. Chance determines our fate at least as profoundly as choice, or these non-existent notions, Karma, qismet, 'destiny'.

It is not the notions that are non-existent, it is the reality of the entities to which they supposedly correspond. The notion of a unicorn exists, but not a unicorn. We all make mistakes, but they are less forgivable in one who prides himself on his command of language.

Throughout the book, one has the impression that Rushdie has always been, and was always entitled to have been, a member of an elite. He grew up in the Karachi of the 1950s and 60s, in an anglicised and freethinking family, such as I doubt exists now, progress being what it is. He has a *le tout Paris* kind of social life, wherever he may happen to be. He appears to have hundreds of friends, which makes my own social circle seem very restricted. Occasionally, however, he feels the need (so I surmise) to be one of the lads. Describing how he walked into a glass door as he accompanied home the woman who was soon to be his wife, he writes:

My head was spinning. "Don't pass out," I instructed myself fiercely. "Do not fucking faint."

This reminded me of my time as a prison doctor when a prisoner would complain, 'I've got this fucking headache.' 'Before we go any further,' I would say, 'can you explain to me the difference between a headache and a fucking headache?'[35]

By the use of the word, Rushdie tries, I surmise, to establish himself as a man of the people, not a man of the elite with thousands of famous or well-heeled friends. He descends to the demotic from time to time in his effort to prove it:

> I tried hard to avoid the elephant-in-the-room cliché, but the unavoidable truth was that there was a fucking enormous mastodon in my workroom, waving its trunk and snorting and stinking quite a bit.

I wanted to ask him what the difference was between an enormous mastodon and a fucking enormous mastodon. I think that the main difference between these two expressions is that the first does not have quite the proletarian quality of the second. If you use the word *fucking* often enough, you show that you are on the side of the underdog, of the insulted and the injured.

Rushdie refers to the deaths of some of his literary contemporaries: Angela Carter, Bruce Chatwin, Raymond

---

[35] There is actually a form of headache brought on by coitus, but this is not what was meant.

Carver, Christopher Hitchens and lastly Martin Amis. 'Death,' he said, 'was showing up at the wrong addresses.'

But what were the right addresses for death to show up at? Hating Donald Trump and Boris Johnson, at one point placing them in a list along with Adolf Eichmann, he implies that death should have called for them instead. Only someone with a completely undisciplined mind would put the three of them in the same list, someone lacking in self-control. And should writers be exempt from death, as they were once exempt from taxes in Ireland?

An interesting section of the book is about the forthcoming trial of his assailant, should he continue to plead 'not guilty' despite having committed his crime in the presence of hundreds. I am unsure of it, but I should imagine that Rushdie is a penological liberal, except in the case of his assailant for whom he desires the maximum sentence. Here I agree with him, of course: I think the man should go to prison for the rest of his life with no possibility of release. And Rushdie is understandably reassured that he will almost certainly receive a sentence far longer than Rushdie's life expectancy. But should others not be similarly reassured when they are the victims of crime?

Rushdie writes something that I think is foolish, though commonplace enough: 'I've heard no regret or remorse from him [the assailant], or through his lawyer, in eight months. That makes him a dangerous man in my book.'

But regret or remorse, so sentimentally valued by judges and others, can be, and often are, faked. Moreover, one can genuinely regret that one has eaten too much, and resolve never to do so again, only to return to the trough in very short order when the opportunity arises. Rushdie is naïve—for a novelist.

Instruction is to be found not only in the best books, the masterpieces of past years, but in quite ordinary ones. The fact is that most books are written by intelligent people and almost always have something to tell us, albeit that they are forgotten within weeks or months of publication—if they are remembered even *that* long.

Thus, I took up, not quite at random, a book by Sir Leo Page, titled *The Young Lag*, published in 1950, the year before his death. He was a barrister and a magistrate and must have been prominent in his day because he was knighted: but he is now so obscure that he does not even have an entry in *Wikipedia*, which is obscurity indeed.

The word 'lag' is no longer current. It suggests to me a prisoner who is habituated to, and comfortable with, life in prison, which alternates, but not necessarily by preference, with spells outside. This is not the meaning given in Eric Partridge's magnificent and astonishingly erudite *A Dictionary of the Underworld, British and American: Being the Vocabularies of Crooks, Criminals, Racketeers, Beggars, and Tramps, Convicts, the Commercial Underworld, the Drug Traffic, the White Slave Traffic, Spivs*, which was ready for publication in the year of my birth, 1949, but not published until 1950 because of the enduring economic effects of the war in Britain[36]. At any rate, between

---

[36] Possibly prolonged by mistaken economic and other policy.

the time of my birth and the time of the word's descent into disuse, its connotation must have changed, for in my recollection the term 'old lag' never meant a former prisoner and nothing else, which is the definition given in the dictionary. The meanings of words change, sometimes quite quickly.

Sir Leo's book, published in the same year as the dictionary's appearance, is well-written, without jargon, and clearly intended to be understood, which is more than can be said for quite a lot of criminological writing today, perhaps to disguise its intellectual nullity. Be that as it may, Sir Leo's procedure is to take the histories of 23 young prisoners who were delinquent in their youth and to try to draw conclusions therefrom. Perhaps the most unfashionable conclusion that he draws is that there is nothing psychologically wrong with them. They are merely (on the whole) not very bright and somewhat lacking in the normal inhibitions, moral and social, that most of us have from stealing from our neighbours or committing other crimes.

Reading the book three quarters of a century after it was published, which I imagine is very rarely done, certain things stand out. Sir Leo is clearly worried by the rapid increase of crime leading up to the writing of his book, but that period now seems almost a golden age of law abidingness by comparison with ours. Alarm about the present depends on comparison with the recent past not with the unknowable future. It is living memory that counts, though of course such memory may be deceptive. That things are better than two hundred years ago will console no one; that they are worse than twenty years ago will alarm anyone old enough to remember.

Certain statistics in the book, by comparison with those of today, are enough to alarm. In 1938, there were 8750 prisoners in Britain, and in 2024 there are very nearly ten times as many, or six times when the growth in the population is taken into account. Nor is this all; there are six times as many indictable offences known per prison in 2024 as there were in 1938. Of course, there are differences in the classification of crimes and in rates of reporting and recording, but I think that these differences would widen rather than narrow the gap. Therefore, it would not be unreasonable to suggest that criminality is at least thirty times as widespread now as it was in 1938, and quite possibly more still. Sir Leo, who is patently a decent man, starts his book by saying (in 1950) how much better criminals were then treated than fifty years before:

> The first forty years of the present century saw such advance as our world would have thought impossible in 1900. It was recognised that the State had been successful in fulfilling its duty entirely only when the offender emerged at the end of his prison sentence a better man than he was at its commencement... It is an immense step forward that so humane and advanced a principle should have received official acceptance.

Even in my time in the prison in which I worked I saw an immense improvement in the material conditions (already much better than they had been shortly before); but improvement in the material conditions, alas, and the supposed improvement in the understanding of the sociological and psychological sources of criminality were not matched by any discernible improvement in any other sense. Sometimes, indeed, it seems that the more a social problem is studied, the worse it gets. The study of addiction is a case in point: I remember reading on the website of the American National Institute on Drug Abuse a self-congratulatory statement to the effect of how much the understanding of addiction had advanced, in large part because of the NIDA's own research, while at the same time an unprecedented number of people were dying of overdoses of drugs of addiction. The operation was a success, but the patient died: as I have mentioned before, supposedly a common saying of nineteenth century surgeons.[37]

Sir Leo does not claim that in psychopathology lies the root of crime. He says, with characteristic clarity such as is not often now to be found on the subject, so that even if he is mistaken one knows what he means:

> That the very great preponderance of law-breakers are not psychologically abnormal is the conclusion to which I have been led, not only by the study of the few young men described in this book, but by experience of the far greater number whom I have met in many years of

---

[37] This attitude was satirised in a little jingle about the eminent British physician of the eighteenth century, John Coakley Lettsom:

My name is John Coakley Lettsom,
I blisters, I bleeds, I sweats 'em.
If after that they choose to die,
Why verily, I lets 'em.

earlier work in prison... To say this is not to deny that there is a small reside of cases which, by the normal standards of human conduct, are inexplicable; nor is it inconsistent with a profound belief that, not only in their own interests but in those of the community as a whole, such exceptional offenders are best treated not by the judge or the gaoler but by the psychologist.[38]

Here I am at one with him, and it seems to me that the claim, often made, that 70 per cent of prisoners are psychiatrically disturbed in some way is a typical means by which work is both created and avoided. It provides an excuse for the gross neglect of those few difficult, sometimes dangerous and volatile lunatics who are in our prisons, because there is supposedly so much other work to do among the 70 per cent.

The crimes of which Sir Leo's subjects were guilty now have a quaintly innocent air about them: with neither drugs nor violence, with theft of bicycles quite common. I do not think, if such a study were repeated today, it would be easy to find cases about whom the following could be written:

There had never been any sort of financial need in the family, and [the young man] was proud of the fact that all of them were very much looked up to by the neighbours. The whole family have always been regular churchgoers, and as a boy [he] himself was regular both

---

[38] By which he also means the psychiatrist.

at church and Sunday school.

In those days, more than half of children attended Sunday school, though belief among parents in God was not very strong.

'Why should I let the toad, *work*, squat on my life?' asked Philip Larkin. Why indeed?

In my case, I would reply that if it were not the toad, work, what other creature would it be? The cockroach, boredom? I cannot think of any better squatter: life has to be lived (barring suicide, of course) and time has to be filled. I am quite fond of my toad, and as it happens, I like non-metaphorical toads also. When I find one in my garden, I pick it up and place it on a dark brown metal table: its expression is always serious and melancholy. It reminds me of a fat and prosperous businessman whose business is beginning to fail, or who suffers from angina and knows that his days are numbered.

I always replace the toad where I found it, and wonder, absurdly, whether it experiences gratitude for me sparing its life. Certainly, it makes little effort to escape, as if it knew that, really, it was safe in my keeping.

I can't help thinking of toads in an anthropomorphic way: as, indeed, even of insects.

Larkin asks himself whether he can't free himself from the necessity to work by the exercise of his intelligence, which would allow him to become rich at a stoke, or alternatively to reduce his need to consume. Plenty of people, he says, neither earn nor spend much money, and 'no one actually *starves*.'

But Larkin has both an internal and an external toad:

> For something superficially toad-like
>> Squats in me, too...

We blame out circumstances for our miseries, but we fashion our circumstances too. Is the toad that squats within us our responsibility? Are we born with such toads, or do we breed them ourselves?

Larkin's poem, *Toads*, was first published in book form in 1955, in a slender volume titled *The Less Deceived*, an obvious reference to Ophelia's piercing reply to Hamlet when he says that he loved her not: 'I was the more deceived.'

Can we be undeceived or disillusioned without first having been deceived or have been under an illusion? A kind of disappointment runs through Larkin's work, as if to be happy were impossible.

> What can be said
> Except that suffering is exact, but where
> Desire takes charge, readings will grow erratic?

No lasting fulfilment is possible, at best the temporary joy of scratching at an itch. In *Wants*, Larkin says (remember he was only 32 at the time):

> Beyond all this, the wish to be alone...
> Beneath it all, desire of oblivion runs:
> Despite the artful tensions of the calendar,

> The life insurance, the tabled fertility rite,
> The costly aversion of the eyes from death—
> Beneath it all, desire of oblivion runs.

I have some slight experience of that desire for oblivion. Sometimes, I come out of my siesta and am depressed to find myself awake. 'Oh no,' I think, 'now I shall have to *do* something.' I try then, unsuccessfully, to return to oblivion, but sleep will not come. Ah, if only I could return to that blissful state of being half-awake, in that dream world that is interesting but not demanding.

Larkin was born in Coventry, as yet un-bombed, now a dreadful place in which I used sometimes to give evidence in murder trials, sometimes for the defence, sometimes for the prosecution. It was one of the finest mediaeval cities in Europe before the war (*coventriser* was once a French verb for the obliteration of a city), but the town council had plans even before the Luftwaffe achieved them of destroying its ancient buildings and of rebuilding it as the semi-Soviet city it is today. In any case Larkin lived in the suburbs, and suburbia is dispiriting. On a train passing through:

> Was that [Coventry],' my friend smiled, 'where you have
>   your roots?'
> No, only where my childhood was unspent,
> I wanted to retort.

An 'unspent childhood'—a brilliant evocation of a spiritless and dispiriting world. Larkin did not think much of Coventry:

'You look as if you wished the place in Hell,'
My friend said, 'judging from your face.' 'Oh well,
I suppose it is not the place's fault,' I said.

A bureaucratic-town-planning sub-hell would now be the best description of it. Once in Coventry for a few days to testify in a trial, I asked the hotel receptionist for the whereabouts of a good restaurant. She suggested one and said that it was seven minutes' walk away, so I said that I would go on foot. 'Oh, I shouldn't do that if I were you,' she said. 'Why not?' I asked. 'Because you would have to take walkways and pedestrian underpasses and they are dangerous after dark.' The muggers and rapists had been thoughtfully concealed from public view by the town-planners. The receptionist said that she would call me a taxi. 'How long will it take in a taxi?' I asked. 'Seven minutes,' she replied. There was no traffic at this time. 'How can it take as long in a taxi as to walk?' I asked. 'Because of the way the road system is built—all those flyovers and overpasses.'

The reason Coventry is not to blame, according to Larkin, is because:

Nothing, like something, happens anywhere.

The desire for events is perpetual, but delusive. Everything signifies nothing.

One of the best and most famous poems in the collection is *Church Going*. It captures very well a kind of nostalgia for an Anglicanism of the past, too weak to oppress, more a kind of social convention with mildly religious overtones, not a church militant: a kindly religion too polite to remind those that did not adhere to its tenets that they were storing up trouble in the Hereafter.

The first lines remind the reader, at least of a certain age, of times more civilised and genteel than his own:

> Once I am sure that there's nothing going on
> I step inside, letting the door thud shut.

Nowadays, churches are locked shut when not in actual use and there are warnings to thieves that there is an alarm system connected to the police station (not that the police would ever come, at least not in time, for you never know, the burglars might be armed).

If there had been a service, it would have embarrassed Larkin, a non-believer. But notwithstanding his unbelief, Larkin recognises that a church, especially an ancient one, hard to maintain for lack of believers, is not just a building like any other:

> A serious house on serious earth it is…
> And that much can never be obsolete,
> Since someone will forever be surprising
> A hunger in himself to be more serious…

I wonder how long it will be before someone in the monstrous regiment of copyeditors changes the line:

> A hunger in himself to be more serious…

to:

A hunger in themself to be more serious.

Making such change is what counts nowadays as being more serious.

I developed a taste early in my life for Chekhov and, unlike many such tastes, it has stayed with me. When I was a young adult, I even bought books *about* Chekhov, a habit that has remained with me, so that I now possess shelvesful of books about his life and work. I have already mentioned the book of Vladimir Yermilov, the Stalinist literary hack whose opinions changed with the ideological winds (in those days, in his defence, opportunism was a matter not only of livelihood but of life and death, so that even silence could be dangerous for anybody who had once spoken). It seems to me that literary criticism in the English-speaking world is moving in an ever more ideological direction, though as yet there is no central authority on high to enforce the orthodoxy *du jour*. It is all the more dispiriting, then, that there should be such an orthodoxy, for this indicates a kind of freely chosen or voluntary servitude, that is to say a servitude without the excuse that it has been enforced by terror or the shadow of the scaffold.[39]

---

[39] This may be in the process of becoming a distinction with very little difference. As I know from several friends who have applied for jobs in universities, at least in departments of humanities, they

I have two sets of the works of Chekhov, the first in the translation of Constance Garnett, and the second in that of Ronald Hingley, which is much more recent. I prefer the first, perhaps through familiarity, and perhaps because I think that having lived through Chekhov's lifetime, though she survived him by 42 years,[40] and having translated him not very long after his death, her English was more likely to approximate his Russian than later translations. Her translations have been criticised by luminaries such as Vladimir Nabokov; and more recently I was surprised by those of David Magarshack, himself a translator from the Russian. He considered Mrs Garnett's knowledge of Russian wasn't really up to translation, and that because of her ignorance of the nuances of the language, she gave English readers a completely false impression of the whole tenor of Chekhov's work. What we consider to be Chekhovian is really Garnettian. Magarshak says, in *The Real Chekhov*, published in 1972:

Chekhov burst upon the English stage at a time when Stanislavsky and his Moscow Art Theatre were at the height of their fame in the West. It was natural, therefore, that Stanislavsky's idea of Chekhov's plays as 'tragedies of Russian life' should have been accepted without question. It was also at the same time—that is, in the

---

must sign up to political or ethical tenets in which they do not believe before their applications can be even considered. They are then faced with a dilemma: either they sign up to them, in which case they feel as if they are careerists, or they do not, in which case they will not be considered for the job. Dissent in such departments is increasingly regarded as crime rather than disagreement.

[40] Anton Chekhov 1860-1904, Constance Garnett 1861-1946.

early twenties—that the only widely recognised translator from the Russian was Constance Garnett, whose admirable zeal and indefatigable perseverance was only equalled by her inadequate knowledge of Russian, which never rose above the dictionary level. It was Constance Garnett who for a long time monopolised the presentation of Chekhov plays on the English stage, leaving a ghastly legacy of misconceptions and misrepresentations that made the playwright synonymous in the mind of the English spectator with sadness, gloom and despair.

I am completely unqualified to comment, having not even a dictionary level of Russian, but I suspect that Magarshack might have been slightly envious that Mrs Garnett got there before him (he was born in 1899 in Riga) and subsequent translators rarely have the same cachet as the first. When I compare Mrs Garnett's translations with Hingley's. I notice changes in word order and sometimes in the words themselves, but the overall impression is much the same. It would be strange if both translators had the faults that Magarshack attributes to Mrs Garnett.[41]

She titles a story *A Doctor's Visit* that Hingley titles *A Case History*. Written in 1898, when Chekhov was 38, one can easily see what a Soviet hack like Yermilov would make of it

The story is simple and the denouement ambiguous. A professor of medicine receives a telegram from Madame

---

[41] Garnett calls her author Tchehov, Magarshack calls him Chekhov.

Lyalikov, the owner of a factory, asking him to pay a visit to her daughter because she is ill. This in itself establishes a sense of privilege: not everyone would think to ask a professor of medicine to pay a visit at some distance. The professor does not go, but sends his assistant (houseman in Hingley's translation, but assistant is better), one Korolyov, instead. Of course, the sense of class privilege would be grist to Yermilov's mill, as if privileges did not exist under the Bolsheviks and the Politburo received exactly the level of medical care as everyone else in the Soviet Union.

Korolyov goes to the factory, adjacent to which live the Lyalikovs, mother and daughter (the father, founder of the business, is dead). As he enters the large premises, the doctor reflects that 'within [factories] there was always sure to be impenetrable ignorance and dull egoism on the side of the owners, wearisome, unhealthy toil on the side of the workpeople, squabbling, vermin, vodka...' This depiction suited Bolshevik historiography perfectly, with a nice neat division, with one class inherently and casually futile, cruel and stupid, and the other with faults entirely attributable to its wretched circumstances not of its choosing, which faults were to be swept away in Yermilov's 'purifying storm', such that the oppressed class would thenceforth live a prosperous, comfortable, cultivated, vodka-free existence.

Miss Lyalikov has nothing more wrong with her than what used to be called a fit of the vapours, brought on by the futility and emptiness of her existence. There is nothing more that Dr Korolyov can do for her that has not already been done by the factory doctor: the latter's very existence surely being a sign of progress or improvement. But Dr Korolyov reflects that, notwithstanding any improvements, everything remains fundamentally the same:

> They may have [musical and theatrical] performances for the workpeople, magic lanterns, factory doctors and improvements of all sorts, but, all the same, the workpeople he had met on his way from the station did not look in any way different from those he had known long ago in his childhood, before there were factory performances and improvements.

Of course, Yermilov would say that this was because the workers did not own the factories, as they would once Soviet power was established.

But there is another passage that would have delighted Yermilov even more. Looking at the factory from the outside as he leaves, Dr Korolyov thinks that there is something baffling about it:

> Fifteen hundred or two thousand workpeople are working without rest in unhealthy surroundings, making bad cotton goods, living on the verge of starvation, and only waking from this nightmare at rare intervals in the tavern... simply that Christina Dmitriyenvna [Miss Lyalikov's governess] may eat sterlet and drink Madeira.

In the end, the doctor concludes that Miss Lyalikov's distress does her credit because she knows that it is unjust that she should be heiress to all this misery, and this awareness is the source of her fit of the vapours.

This matches Bolshevik ideology or apologetics perfectly. But the leap to the conclusion that Chekhov would have approved or rejoiced at the Soviet regime is far beyond preposterous.

I do not in general write in these notebooks twice in succession about the same author—just as most written constitutions with at least a pretence of democratic legitimacy do not allow more than two consecutive terms to a president—but I will make an exception for Chekhov. In the third volume of Constance Garnett's edition of *The Tales of Tchehov*[42,] *The Black Monk* runs from page 103 to page 151. The story was published in 1894, when Chekhov was 34.

The protagonist is Vassilitch Kovrin, an academic philosopher of about Chekhov's age. He is an orphan who has a country property of his own, Kovrinka, but he was largely brought up by a guardian, Yegor Semyonitch Pesotsky, who has a daughter called Tanya. Kovrin goes on an extended summer holiday visit to Pesotsky's estate, there to work on his writing.

Pesotsky is a famous and fanatical horticulturalist, author of books and papers on the subject. His work is his life, and he wants it to continue after his death. The only man he trusts to do so is Kovrin, his former ward, whom he also wants Tanya to marry. Anyone else than Kovrin, he thinks, would simply

---

[42] I am not sure that *Tales* is quite the right word. Stories would be better.

dismember his estate for whatever he could get for it, and the work would cease.

Fortunately—at first—Kovrin and Tanya fall in love and some time later marry. But before long everything turns wretched and ends in tragedy. At first, Kovrin studies hard and writes a lot, but he sleeps very little and is overactive. One evening, Kovrin experiences a visual hallucination:

> From the horizon there rose up to the sky, like a whirlwind or a waterspout, a tall black column. Its outline was indistinct, but from the first instant it could be seen that it was not standing still, but moving with fearful rapidity, moving straight toward Kovrin, and the nearer it came the smaller and more distinct it was.

It resolved itself into a monk dressed in black. It should be mentioned here that Kovrin had previously been reflecting on a legend of a Black Monk a thousand years old, according to which he would return to earth at just about this time. I was reminded of a passage from De Quincey: 'If a man whose talk is of oxen should become an opium-eater, the probability is, that... he will dream of oxen: whereas in the case before him, the reader will find that the Opium-eater [that is to say, De Quincey himself] boasteth himself to be a philosopher.' In other words, psychotic phenomena bear some relation to the previous content of people's minds.

And so it proves with the Black Monk.

> There came out noiselessly, without the slightest rustle, a man of medium height with uncovered grey hair, all in

black, and barefooted like a beggar, and his black eyebrows stood out on his pale, death-like face. Nodding his head graciously, this beggar or pilgrim came noiselessly to the seat and sat down, and Kovrin recognised him as the Black Monk.

'The legend,' said the Monk, 'the mirage and I are all the products of your imagination. I am a phantom.'

'Then you don't exist,' said Kovrin.

'You can think what you like,' said the monk with a faint smile. 'I exist in your imagination, and your imagination is part of nature, so I exist in nature.'

The Black Monk goes on to persuade Kovrin that he, Kovrin, is someone special, 'you are the one of those few who are justly called the chosen of God.'

Kovrin exults. He now believes himself to be a genius. He declares his love for Tanya who, participating in his belief as if by contagion[43], believes him to be a great man also.

One long winter evening, however, Tanya wakes to see Kovrin, her husband, talking to his visual hallucination that has reappeared to him in their bedroom.

Tanya woke up, and looked with amazement and horror at her husband. He was talking, addressing the armchair [in which he saw the Black Monk sitting], laughing and gesticulating; his eyes were gleaming and there was

---

[43] There is a condition, *folie à deux*, in which a sane person comes to believe the delusions of a person to whom he or she is very close. When they are separated, the former loses his or her belief in the other person's delusion.

something strange in his laugh.

To cut a long story short, Kovrin is suffering from delirium. At the end of the story, he dies of tuberculosis, his life in ruins.

In the meantime, he has been given potassium bromide as a tranquilliser, the only effective such drug in his day, and it does indeed suppress his hallucinations. What astonishes me about the story is its clinical accuracy: I was accustomed to supposing that doctors in Chekhov's time knew very little because they could do very little. This is a *non sequitur*, of course, and without their knowledge the subsequent therapeutic advances could hardly have been made.

Visual hallucinations, unlike auditory ones, are usually or most commonly a symptom of delirium brought about by fever or other illness. Lishman's great textbook, *Organic Psychiatry*, whose nine hundred pages of closely-printed text I read with pleasure from cover to cover when it was first published in 1978, eight-four years after *The Black Monk*, says of visual hallucinations, *inter alia*:

> The reality of the phenomena is fully accepted by the patient who may participate and react accordingly, usually with fear and alarm, but sometimes with interest or even amusement.[44]

But while Kovrin's visual hallucinations ceased under

---

[44] I had difficulty in persuading the hospital management that patients with delirium tremens (from alcohol withdrawal) should be nursed on the ground floor because of their tendency to jump out of windows to escape their frightening visual hallucinations.

bromide treatment, he suffered other consequences. Lishman's description of bromide intoxication fits exactly Kovrin's state and complaints:

> The patient is dull and somnolent, with slowed ideation, disorientation and faulty memory... Irritability, resentment and insomnia are often marked.

Kovrin complains, as do many psychiatric patients under treatment who have experienced periods of exultation in the course of their illness, as follows:

> 'How fortunate Buddha, Mahomed, and Shakespeare were that their kind relations and doctors did not cure them of their ecstasy and their inspiration,' said Kovrin. 'If Mahomed had taken bromide for his nerves, had worked only two hours out of the twenty-four, and had drunk milk, that remarkable man would have left no more trace after him than his dog. Doctors and kind relations will succeed in stupefying mankind, in making mediocrity pass for genius and in bringing civilization to ruin...'

The change in Kovrin under the influence of bromide from a brilliant, active and kindly to a querulous, indolent and unpleasant man hastens his father-in-law's death and wrecks his marriage to Tanya. He goes to live in the Crimea (a place of recuperation for the tuberculous, such as did Chekhov himself) with another woman, Varvara Nikolaevna, and stops taking his bromide. Before long the Black Monk reappears to him in his delirium. He believes once more that he is a genius. He calls out to Tanya as he dies, hallucinating the gardens of her father's estate, and dies of a pulmonary haemorrhage, 'a blissful smile... set on his face.'

I recall a nun who, believing that she was dying, woke in a state of delirium and believed she had ascended to heaven—which is rarely how hospital wards in National Health Service hospitals are experienced. And I recall another patient who had General Paralysis of the Insane, who, while dying, called out for her husband, 'Bill! Bill! Bill!', who never came to visit. Her voice rings in my ears still, and there was no blissful smile on her face when she died.

One of the great pleasures of being a writer is that of being sent books by people you don't know and have never heard of. It is implicitly flattering, for it means that they must consider your good opinion worth having, and in my case the flattery must be sincere because my opinion is commercially useless to them. Of course, it is an especially great pleasure if a book sent you is good and you do not have to resort to faint praise in order to remain both polite and honest.

Shortly after I had re-read Chekhov's *The Black Monk*, I received through the post a slender volume of poems by Mr Reagan Upshaw. Mr Upshaw is an art dealer and critic whose art criticism has appeared in such august journals as the *Washington Post* and the *San Francisco Chronicle* and I assumed, therefore, that his poems would be at least literate. To my great pleasure, I found that they were a good deal better than that.

His book, *In the Panhandle: Poems 1975-2020* is 113 pages long, with not a few blank pages. I think one might conclude from this at least one of the following: that he is not prolific as a poet, or that he has self-effacing discrimination as to which poems he thinks worth re-printing in book form.

He was born and raised in Texas and is or was an art dealer in New York, itself a remarkable trajectory, and in my opinion his poetry has the remarkable ability to distil poetically very different landscapes and social environments. He is also an excellent poet of aging and death, those hardy perennials of poetry: indeed, one might almost say the *sine qua non* (or, as the father of one of my friends put it, the *without-which-not*) of poetry.

Let me begin with Texas. I have been there only once, a long time ago, and its flat landscape impressed me very much—unfavourably. I was in a bar in a little town in Texas when a Texan, discovering that I was English and therefore from Europe, remarked proudly that Texas was larger than the whole of Europe: to which I replied, perhaps rashly, that there was more beauty in one square yard of Europe than in the whole of Texas.

I have since matured and realised that everywhere, taken in the right spirit, is interesting and in its way beautiful: and certainly, Texans are not uninteresting, a breed apart. I think, though, that Mr Upshaw is a breed apart from a breed apart, as perhaps poets are everywhere. Here is the Texan landscape, exactly as I remember it:

It seemed that every native thing grew thorns

on my uncle's ranch—mesquite, cacti, goathead stickers.
Out back, beyond the barbed wire
that circled the house, a tiny stream
trickled from puddle to puddle,
belaboured by sun and incessant wind...

Then:

One year, my uncle told me,
When even the stingy rainfall did come,
the stream failed completely, and
—Who would have thought it?—
he found fish on its sand, little fish,
dead and dried up. Whoever dreamed
something could have loved in there?

To which he adds laconically, 'Or in here?'
Could any few lines capture a landscape, and even the
hardships and difficulties that it imposes on those who live in
it, better than these? Suddenly, one feels a deep respect for his
uncle, for to wrest a livelihood from such a place is a triumph
of the spirit.

Another poem brilliantly catches the pathos of young men
killed in car accidents (or by suicide) along the Texas roads,
the place where they happened marked by crude memorial
crosses:

After the bloodstained wrecks are towed away,
reports are filed, and funerals are held,
we often see, like mushrooms after rain,

these humble roadside crosses springing up
amid the shards of glass and mangled bolts,
white-painted crossbars trussed or tacked together
and garlanded with artificial flowers.

They are crude, these crosses; sometimes they have names painted on them, sometimes not, though mere names tell us nothing anyway. But the crosses outlast more formal tombstones that quickly wear down to intelligibility and are not even visited, whereas at least these crosses:

flicker in the memories of those
who pass them daily, modest evidence
of love and loss, and finally, just love.

As I have mentioned, Mr Upshaw is good on death; he almost reconciles us to it, as being the precondition of a meaningful life. He evidently had a difficult time with his mother when he was a child:

When I'm with an angry woman
I'm home...
but the anger of women has been
a passion I could count on, that moment
when the eyes widen, the smile
is sucked in. Then the belt came down;
now fingernails claw for my face,
pots and glasses whiz through the air.
I dodge or cajole, and in that moment
I know where I am.

One never forgets the cruelties experienced in childhood, but one does not dwell on them. Forgetting is not the mere inability to remember; it is often a conscious decision to do so.

Many years later, Mr Upshaw's mother suffered from Alzheimer's disease. His poem, *Alzheimer's*, begins with as moving an evocation of this terrible condition as I daresay has ever been written:

> Each day my mother in her wheelchair bends
> A hair's breadth closer to a fetal pose.
> Her staring eyes are vacant, and her hands
> fold like a baby's on to nothing. Nose
> to nose, cajoling, my sad father keeps
> performing love's last duty twice a day:
> to hold her death at bay
> by spooning mush through her indifferent lips.

There is as good a poem about the death of his father, a doctor, which raises the question of whether it is better to die of a sudden, or to linger to say one's goodbyes (a question increasingly less abstract for me, though not finally one for me to decide):

> Alas, we know all too well
> that a little noticed
> unheroic, drug-assisted slide
> into nothing
> is the destiny that probably awaits us.

I have not done justice to Mr Upshaw's surprising range in

so short a compass, for justice cannot always be done in a few lines or paragraphs. I can only say that I have rarely received an unsolicited book with so much pleasure and gratitude.

The differences between projection, prediction and prophecy are important and perhaps everyone is fully conversant with them—though I have in my time not only mistaken the one for the other but done so in print.

In 1982, for example, when I visited Egypt for the first time, I learned a statistic that the population growth meant that one per cent of Egypt's cultivable land per annum, irrigated by the Nile, was being built over. Since food supplies were already precarious, I confidently predicted famine would stalk the land—famine that forty years later has yet to happen.[45]

I had projected a single factor and measure and turned it into a prophecy. It was a prophecy rather than a prediction because I placed no date upon its fulfilment, by which it might come to be known as true or false. If I had said that by the year 1999, say, Egypt would know famine, it would have been a prediction, but a false one. With my prophecy, it is still open to me to say that there has been no famine *yet*, but that it will come...

We all love a good prophecy, provided it is of disaster or apocalypse. True, after the apocalypse everything is hoped to

---

[45] I do not mean to imply that all is well and Egypt is without its difficulties.

turn out well, but the perfection that is to be wrought by it is so psychologically remote that it has no purchase on our mind. Thus the prophet Marx, who took himself and was taken by others to be a scientist (in his latter years, he definitely looked like a prophet, rather an implacable one) prophesied a final class war that was real enough in people's minds, while the endless cruise afterwards aboard the ship, the M.V. *Classlessness*, or on its sister ship, the M.V. *Withering-away-of-the-State*, was etiolated to the point of non-existence.

In the year of my father's birth, 1909, E.M. Forster published what as far I know was his only foray into the genre of science fiction—and a brilliant one it was too. I thought of it because, a few days before writing this, some fault in a computer program update incapacitated about 3,000,000 computers worldwide, leading to the cancellation of trains, flights, hospital appointments, operations, and so forth. Millions of people were inconvenienced. The error in the update was not malicious (as far as we have been told) but it was a symptom of, and perhaps a warning against, the degree to which we have become dependent on a structure of whose working we have not the faintest understanding.

Forster's story was titled *The Machine Stops* and is set in the indefinite but far future. It could be called prophetic: without a date for its denouement, which is symbolic rather than literal, it depicts an increasingly impersonal and depersonalised world. The story is not fully consistent, but it would be pedantic to demand total consistency of a prophetic story.

In *The Machine Stops*, most of mankind lives singly, underground in monastic-type cells, also resembling those of a beehive. Almost all communication between people is by remote electronic screen and face-to-face contact is eschewed, feared and deprecated almost as disgusting, and certainly as unnecessary. All vital necessities, from food to entertainment, are delivered automatically, at the press of a button, though no one knows from where. The tutelary organisation is called *The Machine*, but its existence is shadowy and no one knows where, exactly, it is located. It has a Central Committee like a revolutionary party (remember, Forster wrote this eight years before the Bolshevik Revolution), but no one knows of whom it consists or how members are chosen—or even if it exists in reality. This is Kafka *avant la lettre*, all the more surprising in an author who has more in common with Jane Austen than with, say, Robert Heinlein.

Most of us feel that our lives are influenced if not controlled by shadowy organisations of whose working we have little knowledge or conception, and those who do not feel it have simply failed to think about it.

Vashti and her son Kuno are the two main—or only—characters in the story. Reproduction in this future world requires the permission of The Machine and children are taken into public nurseries soon after birth. (There is no talk of Kuno's father, as if it were an irrelevant datum, and there is nothing romantic about human reproduction, which presumably is now a purely technical procedure.)

It is odd, then, that Kuno should still be in contact with his mother, at least electronically. This is an inconsistency in the story. Kuno has been allocated a cell in the northern hemisphere whereas Vashti's is in the southern. There persists some slight emotional relationship between the two.

Kuno announces to his mother over the screen, which is remarkably like an iPad, that he wishes to visit the surface of the Earth. This wish seems bizarre, even perverse, to Vashti. The air unmediated by The Machine's ventilation system is now deemed to be dangerous: moreover, permission to visit the surface requires a good reason for it to be granted. But Kuno decides to go ahead without such permission. He wants his mother to visit him physically before he embarks on his adventure, which is another bizarre or perverse idea on his part. Such a visit is made possible, though not encouraged, by the existence of airship travel at great speed (actually slower than ordinary air travel today). Vashti takes one of these airships but *en route* deliberately blacks out the windows, for the sun, the stars and the surface of the earth hold no interest for her and even appear almost disgusting.

There are passages in *The Machine Stops* that are prescient. Near the beginning of the story, we read about Vashti in her cell:

> An electric bell rang…
> "I suppose I must see who it is," she thought…
> "Who is it?" she called. Her voice was irritable, for she had been interrupted often since the music [which she had selected electronically] began. She knew several thousand people, in certain directions human intercourse had advanced enormously.

In certain directions human intercourse had advanced enormously: who could fail to recognise this as our modern predicament or paradox, especially that of the young, the so-called digital natives, who spend far more of their time in virtual than in real contact with their fellows, and who have huge numbers of distant acquaintances without really knowing anyone. The lonely crowd is a tête-à-tête by comparison.

When Vashti discovers that it is her son, she says to him, 'I do not expect anything important to happen in the next five minutes—I can give you fully five minutes, Kuno.'

Five minutes is a long time in a world of constant messaging—such as ours. A whole five minutes for her son! But Vashti has soon to deliver a lecture lasting the customary ten minutes (a prescient commentary on out decreasing attention span):

> The clumsy system of public gatherings had long since been abandoned; neither Vashti nor her audience stirred from their rooms. Seated in her armchair she spoke, while they in their armchairs heard her, fairly well, and saw her, fairly well.

A Zoom meeting, then.

Eventually The Machine, or perhaps the mechanism, begins to break down and humanity is helpless because for years it has done nothing, produced nothing, for itself.

A prophetic prophecy, then: but what good are such prophecies?

A friend of mine, who shares my interest in criminal

poisonings (though his interest is largely professional, unlike mine, which is mainly prurient) came to stay at our house in France and spent much of his time in what I may call, without exaggerating or boasting, my library, which has a larger number than average of books on this arcane subject.

We discussed Victorian flypaper murders, that is to say those murders, or alleged murders, committed by the culprit by soaking arsenic-containing flypapers and dosing the victim with the resulting fluid. There were Catherine Flanagan and Margaret Higgins, Mrs Maybrick (mentioned in James Joyce's *Ulysses*) and Frederick Seddon to discuss. My friend had a theory that Seddon, who was hanged, was innocent and that it was his wife who was guilty of the crime of poisoning their lodger. Mrs Seddon arranged things to make her hateful husband look guilty and thus disembarrass herself of him by means of the scaffold. Certainly, she remarried soon after he was executed, but there are nevertheless objections to this theory, intriguing as it is.

Quite by chance, I was leafing soon after our discussion through a book of short stories by the novelist, Elizabeth Taylor, when I came across her story, *The Fly-Paper*. It was in the collection titled *The Devastating Boys*, published in 1972, which I had long possessed but not read—for a strange reason. I had read her novel, *Mrs Palfrey at the Claremont*, published the year before this collection of stories, and I was reluctant to read anything else by her because I had so admired it and feared that reading anything else by her would be a disappointment.

The Fly-Paper is short, a mere nine pages—and those not very closely-printed. It conveys menace and hints at the commission of a hideous crime to come, all without lingering on lurid detail.

A girl called Sylvia, aged eleven, travels on a bus outside a small town to her piano lesson with an unpleasant teacher who has a bad piano and lives in a dingy house. Sylvia herself is not an attractive girl and has no talent for music. She goes to the lesson because her grandmother insists on it, her mother being dead. Sylvia is early for her lesson and will have to fill in half an hour before it.

Opposite her on the bus to the lesson is a tall, bald man who, unwanted by her, soon engages her in conversation. When he learns that she is on her way to a music lesson and that her name is Sylvia, he begins to sing Schubert's setting of *Who Is Sylvia?* (which establishes him as a man of some culture). His singing evokes the displeasure of a woman on the bus, who seems a kindly and protective person. When the man says to her, 'I take it, Madam, that you do not appreciate my singing?' she replies, 'I should think it's hardly the place, that's all.'

When Sylvia gets off the bus, the man to whom she has taken a dislike because of his insidious friendliness gets off too. He offers her an ice-cream from a nearby shop, but before she can answer the woman on the bus, who has also alighted, intervenes. 'Haven't you ever been told not to talk to strangers?' she asks, and she takes Sylvia in hand, accompanying her as she walks. 'You should *never*,' she says, adding, 'There's some funny people about these days.'

The woman takes her by a different route, by some gravel pits (a good place for the disposal of bodies, though this is kept strictly implicit in the story). As they walk together, they can see the man behind them, and the woman says, 'Oh, it's disgraceful, and with all the things you read in the papers. You can't be too careful, and you'll have to remember that in future. I'm not sure I ought not to inform the police.'

Sylvia, still early for her lesson, and afraid to knock early on the teacher's door, accepts the woman's offer to come into her house for 'a nice cup of tea'.

The house is neat and uncluttered, unlike her grandmother's and her music teacher's house. There is a budgerigar in a cage, of which the woman says, 'That's my baby boy, my little Joey,' capturing precisely the sentimentality of evil persons. In the window hangs a flypaper, 'Some of the flies were half alive, and striving helplessly to free themselves. But they were caught forever.' Then, as Sylvia looks at the flypaper, she hears some footsteps on the path to the front door. She 'listened in surprise; but the woman did not seem to hear, or lift her head.'

Continuing to spoon tea from the caddy into the teapot, she calls out, 'Just in time, Herbert,' and the man in the bus enters. 'Well done, Mabel,' he says, closing the door behind him. Sylvia is a fly caught on flypaper.

This brilliant little story, adapted for television in 1980, is economical in its evocation of evil. What will happen—be done—to Sylvia is left to the imagination, where it is all the more horrible for not being said or described.

Life imitates art (alas, in this case). A little later, a couple, Frederick and Rosemary West enticed young women to their house in Gloucester (Rosemary playing the role of Mabel in the story), there to rape, sexually torture and murder their victims. Though of lower social class and lesser education than Herbert and Mabel, their *modus operandi* was similar. The

Wests committed their first murder the year after the book containing *The Fly-Paper* was published, though Fred West was not a man to have read such refined literature.

I was on duty for the prison when West hanged himself. I had met him only a couple of times, for the briefest of medical consultations. He was polite and smiling—this was very shortly before he hanged himself—but I thought there was something were-wolfish about him, though of course I knew he was a serial killer who had buried his victims in his own house, so that my observation was not entirely objective. I used to see him playing pool happily with the prison officers: a strange recompense for having raped and killed, as it is now thought, more than twelve young women, including his own offspring. His wife had a nose, for vulnerable young women who needed shelter for the night.

When West hanged himself, cheering broke out in the prison (his presence gave the other prisoners a bad name). I thought of the poem Siegfried Sassoon wrote to celebrate the Armistice:

> Everyone suddenly burst out singing;
> And I was filled with such delight
> As prisoned birds must find in freedom...

As to flypapers, we sometimes employ them in the house— I don't think they contain arsenic any longer—and I am not proud to say that not only do I rejoice when a fly lands on one of them but I derive a certain sadistic pleasure in watching the fly's futile efforts at escape. Of course, flies torment me, but this is no excuse for my malevolence.

I have come once again very nearly to the end of my notebook, and for the third time (for this is the third of my notebooks) I feel duty bound to write something concerning the furnisher of my title, Dylan Thomas.

This time, however, I shall remark on the life rather than on the work, in particular his relations with his wife, Caitlin Macnamara. I veer between finding her on the one hand irritating to the point of anger and even disgust, and on the other I feel a deep sympathy with, and even for, her. She was a drinker, self-indulgent, bad-tempered, and a hell-raiser because she liked the resultant hell. In her book, written four years after Dylan died, she wrote disdainfully of the people who criticised her conduct (which she allows was pretty dreadful much of the time), for whom 'there is no worse sin than the flouting of convention.'

It is certainly true that mere convention is not enough to guide us through life, and can be very stifling, and even supportive of evil. But let us reverse the valency of her statement and consider the following: 'There is no worse sin than the following of convention.'

This was very much the attitude, when she was young, of Caitlin Thomas, and she took her husband with her—he having a conventional side as well as an instinctive bohemianism. She says of herself, in her overblown, self-dramatising way:

Does the perversity of my nature now dare complain

244

that: having carefully and methodically cut off all family ties, deliberately antagonised friends; and made myself generally as intractable, offensive, violent, and as similar to an infuriated wild boar from the horniest jungle as I know how, and that is something I do know about—that I am ostracized? That nobody loves me? It does.

To be against convention *as such* is to set oneself up as superior to all those around one who stick to it, and to proclaim oneself some kind of moral, intellectual or artistic genius. As is often the way, Doctor Johnson has something useful to say on this matter. In his life of Jonathan Swift, he remarks on Swift's 'singularity', but goes on to say that he who keeps to convention is better than he who flouts it, *unless he be better*.

The latter is an all-important rider. Doctor Johnson does *not* say that convention is an infallible guide to good conduct, but suggests that most people require it, though it is possible to rise above it by means of honest reflection, thought and courage.

The same is true of much orthodoxy. It is not enough in the search for truth to oppose orthodoxy, though finding the truth may mean the abandonment of orthodoxy, even a highly cherished orthodoxy.

In short, judgment is needed, and Caitlin Thomas, for much of her life, had very little of it. If she wasn't herself a *poète maudit*, she was the wife of one, and played up to it. I think she would have been what is colloquially known as *a pain in the neck*.

Why, then, do I feel anything like sympathy, even deep sympathy, for her? Why not mere irritation and have done with it?

He who has visited the Boat House in Laugharne where the Thomases lived, will at once realise that life there could not have been easy. Although its outlook is very beautiful (now somewhat spoiled by the erection in what might be called the social-democratic style of houses on the brow of a hill), to have brought up three children there, as did she, without the assistance of modern labour-saving devices, with an unreliable and frequently absent and lionised husband, must have been difficult for one who believed herself to be of artistic bent and talent: a constant round of cooking and washing (admittedly with long visits to the pub), all in cramped and not very comfortable conditions.

But this is not the main reason for my sympathy. Caitlin was ten months older than Dylan, nearly forty when widowed. She went to Italy to start a new life after his death, and eventually, at the age of 48, had a child by an Italian with whom she spent the rest of her life. She sobered up, attended Alcoholics Anonymous, and became more or less respectable. She died aged 80, in the forty-first year of her widowhood (she never married the Italian).

Somewhat surprisingly, in view of the fact that her relationship with the latter lasted much longer than her marriage to Dylan, and that she had a son by him who was in his twenties when she died, she wanted to be buried next to Dylan in Laugharne churchyard—and was so buried. There is something both noble and tragic in this, tragic perhaps for the two Italian men who must have thought that they were *faute de mieux* in her life, and also because she must have carried within her for more than half her lifetime the deep wound of Dylan's early death.

The tombs of both Dylan and Caitlin are deeply moving, a simple white cross with their names and dates of birth and death. They were, as the cant phrase has it, *reunited at last.*

The fact is that, however badly they may have behaved to one another, their love was deep. They were young and immature, and their love took root in the soil of romanticism. That Caitlin's love for Dylan endured, and was the love of her life, I have no doubt. The title of her book published in 1957, four years after his death, *Leftover Life to Kill,* suggests total desolation; and overwritten as it is, the real love, the real grief, shines through:

> He said he loved me; that I was the only woman for him; and, whatever the evidence to the contrary, I believed him and still do; and I am grateful for that bit of faith.

Theirs was a tragedy, one of their own making perhaps; but like all real tragedy, it exerts, at least on me, a cathartic effect.